ON A PIT

Readers are encouraged to go to www.MissionPointPress.com
to contact the author or to find information on how to buy this
book in bulk at a discounted rate.

Published by Mission Point Press
2554 Chandler Rd.
Traverse City, MI 49686
(231) 421-9513
www.MissionPointPress.com

ISBN: 978-1-943995-75-2
Library of Congress Control Number: 2018945518

Printed in the United States of America.

On a Pit & a PRAYER

How I Grew a Business,

Lost a Business,

and Found Faith, Family and Love

Michelle White

MISSION POINT PRESS

To God, my husband, children and family ... thank you for loving me!

Contents

Foreword

I AM DEEPLY HONORED AND HUMBLED TO WRITE this foreword for Michelle. Michelle has impressed me with her honesty and integrity through the many years we have been together. These qualities have allowed Michelle to take the higher road in her journey. Michelle is a fighter for what is right and an advocate for the underdog.

Michelle is a unique and humble human being who has used her life experiences to bring her to this point in time, and her journey is far from over.

As you go on this journey with Michelle, I believe you will find scenarios relevant to your own life. I hope this book brings you a sense of peace when thinking about past experiences that may continue to trouble you, and also provide insight for challenging future experiences.

> Jeremiah 29:11
> *"For I know the plans I have for you," declares the LORD, "plans to prosper you and not to harm you, plans to give you hope and a future."*
> New International Version (NIV)

> Proverbs 3:5-6
> *Trust in the Lord with all thine heart; and lean not unto thine own understanding. In all thy ways acknowledge him, and he shall direct thy path.*
> King James Version (KJV).

— Bill White

*D*OWN THE ROAD. I THINK THAT'S SLANG FOR "I'M FINISHED." "DONE FOR." "RUINED."

Weird to be so fixated on those three words at this dark, dark moment. And yet, I know exactly why they popped into my head.

It's because they're true.

They're emotionally true, but they're also frighteningly close to being geographically true.

Okay, so I'm not literally skidding down the road, but I am parked on the side of it.

Highway I-465 circles Indianapolis like a fifty-mile-long noose, writhing with traffic, even in this pouring rain. The drivers whipping by seem so full of purpose while I just feel numb. And so very far from home.

I wish I was driving M-22 instead of parked in this wet asphalt wasteland. I used to love that dual-lane Michigan road. I used to think M-22 was magic, the way it wound through the most beautiful countryside I'd ever seen. How it took me to all the people who mattered the most, and all the places I knew the best. I close my eyes. It's sunny and warm on M-22. And I picture the freshwater beaches, the sweeping views of Lake

Michigan, the little towns, and my favorite art galleries. Then I picture the homes I lived in with people I love. I've lived here since I was twelve and know these roads and the people that drive them. The house on the corner lot in Leland where Bill, James, Randy, Sam, and I were a family. The land I'd like to turn into a farm and where my parents helped me build my business. And of course, the cherry orchards. Hundreds of them spread over the north like ruby rings on Michigan's hand.

I will myself not to think about any of it. Not to think about my sons, or Bill, or my parents. Not to think about how disappointed in me they must feel. I will myself not to think about art, or how much I love to paint, or about beach days with my family, or about the cherry orchards. I especially will myself not to think about the orchards. I had such plans.

If my goal was to help other people through my business, then why is my own life in constant turmoil? If my goal was to show other people how to be healthy, why do I continue to be so self-destructive? I know that stress is the problem . . . drinking is my way to disappear from it.

I've hurt the people I love the most. My relationship with Bill is a mess. I have goals and dreams, but I am not fulfilling them. My boys need me, and I'm not always there for them. And now, my business is failing. The business I built, and sacrificed for, and that took time away from my family, is failing. I'm not sure I'm strong enough to keep feeling all this pain. I'm truly not sure.

Relief is just outside this car door. It's rush hour, and people with purpose and appointments and goals are speeding by in their shiny SUVs and their sleek sports cars. They drive too fast and don't watch where they're going. I'm a step away from making the pain go away.

All I'd have to do is put one foot in front of the other.

All I'd have to do is open the door and step out of my car.

That's all I'd have to do.

I've got on my Leland Cherry Company jacket. At least they'd know I went down fighting.

· ·

That sad scene happened nearly two decades ago. And obviously, I didn't do it. I didn't step out into traffic on I-465 in front of some poor, unsuspecting motorist.

Instead, I kept my hands on the steering wheel, I kept my car door closed, I put my foot on the accelerator, merged safely into the flow of cars, and no one was the wiser.

But how I got myself to a place so low, and then found the will to keep going, is a story I need to tell. One that started years before I ever found myself sitting alone by the side of that highway. My life is so full now; it's become difficult for me to even imagine I thought once of ending it. But I really think I might have.

· ·

What follows is my experience in building a business—from a seed of an idea to package tart cherry juice concentrate as a revolutionary, natural medicine, to a $1.5 million company with national distribution. It took sixteen tumultuous years. I would travel around the country, appear on television, and earn numerous awards for this business. Looking at it from the outside, it seemed successful. In fact, my story details how ill prepared I was to grow and run it, and the many, many painful lessons I learned along the way. It is a valuable and telling tale of the minefields that await any business startup—and a lesson in why success requires more than simply a good idea and the will to see it through. Success also requires the need for continual financing, positive cash flow, cost management, marketing—plus the importance of trusting others and adjusting right away if that trust is violated. More than anything, it's a lesson in self-awareness and self-evaluation. Know your strengths; know your weaknesses; know how to exploit the former and shore up the latter. I wish someone had told me all that.

And yet, I take full responsibility for my decisions—the productive ones, and the misguided ones, too—that contributed to my company's roller-coaster existence.

This book is much, much more than just a tale of business, though. There are life lessons throughout, learned from my personal struggles as a wife, a mother, and a woman.

In fact, the biggest lesson I've learned has nothing to do with business and money at all, and everything to do with things vastly more important: family, love, and self-respect.

....

Ultimately, what stopped me from stepping out of my car that day in Indiana was faith. Faith in God, faith in love, and—even—faith in myself.

I didn't acquire my faith easily. It took work and hardship and love. But today, when I put those three words together—work, hardship, love—I know they make a much more interesting story than those other three words . . . Down, The, Road.

And boy, am I ever glad I'm living to tell it.

Good Soil

1997 - 1999

"**Y**OU'RE IN LA LA LAND, MICHELLE."

"Get your head out of the clouds, Michelle."

"Geez, Michelle, you're living in a dream world."

People have been saying things like that to me for about as long as I can remember. It used to hurt my feelings, especially when it came from ex-husband or from my mom or my dad. I think they all meant well, but I could never understand what was so bad about taking a little time out of every day for daydreaming. I mean, if a person doesn't have dreams, what do they have to live for? Not that anyone ever asks, but my opinion is, without dreams, our lives might pass us by before we get anywhere or accomplish anything.

It's early in the morning. And for me that's always been the best time to just sit and let your mind wander. The boys are still sleeping, I don't have to be at work for two full hours, and even though my life isn't going exactly how I planned, this is the time of day when my dreams seem close by. When they seem achievable, even if I'm not sure what the specifics of them are yet.

My divorce from my ex is official, and using his recent tone of voice as a guide, I'm pretty sure the man who used to love me now hates me. I'm living with our boys in my parents' dinky rental, I'm broke, and I don't exactly have a job that lets me be creative. (I'm working as an accounts payable and payroll clerk at a cherry processing plant.) These things all weigh on me, but I know they are temporary. The steps that brought me here seem random now but are sure to lead me to my life's purpose. And it will be something great.

It's hardly clear yet what that purpose will be. I know I want to help people. I know I want to express myself. I know I want to eventually have my own business—again, it's not clear what kind of business, but I also know I want it to help people live healthier lives. I also know I wouldn't have figured even that much out if I didn't, as my dad says, have my head in the clouds sometimes. Okay, a lot of the time.

This is how I envision my life:

I will build a pole barn for my business right here on my parents' land. I will grow a lot of my own food, and have a wonderful place for my toddler sons, Sam and Randy, to grow up. I will get along better with my ex, now that we are not married. I will be out of debt. Bill will not just be the man I am dating, he will be the love of my life and we will be together forever. And finally, I will have a successful business and a successful life!

I can see it all, I believe in it, and I will make it happen.

Just as soon as I figure out what's for breakfast.

The boys are awake now, and I can tell by their still sleepy sighs they're about to start crying. The inside of our refrigerator is an empty hole, and payday isn't for three days. Time to get my focus back down to earth. Even I know you can't explain dreams to youngsters like my sons. Especially hungry ones.

....

Here's something I bet you didn't know. In order to redeem food stamps at your local purveyor of provisions—i.e. a corporate, super-center-chain-grocery store—you need to keep said food stamps firmly attached to the coupon book in which you received them. This wisdom is delivered to me verbally, via a blue-haired, underweight, aging cashier with an impressively large silver unibrow.

After work, and after picking up Sam and Randy from day-care, I convince the twins that a shopping trip to a local big box store will be something fun the three of us can do together. If you behave, I tell them, if you don't grab things off the shelves, or fight with each other, you'll get to help me pick out our groceries, and maybe I'll even get you both a treat when we are finished shopping. Which, for the first time in my life, I will do with food stamps. It hurts to even say those words but I didn't really have a choice, and so I filled out the paperwork weeks ago: Yes, I had two kids. Yes, they were only four years old. No, I couldn't afford to feed them and pay for daycare without help. Yes, I was dying of shame, thank you very much.

Now I've finally received my first book of food stamps in the mail. In my mind, that made my current address, "Food Stamp Land." A place I never thought I'd visit, yet alone live, but that's where I am . . . living in Food Stamp Land. In this world I'm raising my twins separately from their dad, I'm an adult who's living with her parents, and I need to ask the government for help to even do that.

Opening the mail and finding the book of food stamps in my mailbox was not exactly a banner day for me. But now we are going shopping. And I am going to buy steak and chicken and eggs and milk and fresh vegetables and fresh fruit and frozen pizza and yogurt and butter and cereal. The refrigerator and the cupboards in my tiny kitchen will be full of food, and I will make those groceries last for a very long time. Or at least until I can figure something else out.

That was the plan anyway. Maybe not a good plan, but a plan nonetheless.

And it might have worked, too, except that I never got a

chance to put it into action. What came next was the box-store cashier with the cold demeanor and the hairy eyebrow. And she was frowning that eyebrow. Hard. At me.

"I can't take those," she tells me, gesturing to my food stamps after I'd wheeled my full cart of groceries into her line and piled them on the conveyor belt.

"What do you mean you can't take them?" I ask, feeling my face catch fire with shame. In a hopeless and preemptive effort to camouflage my payment method from other nearby shoppers, I'd torn the food stamps out of the booklet and put them in my wallet as if they were ten-dollar bills. But the jig was up. Unibrow found me out. And Sam and Randy must have noticed the tone of panic in my voice, because a minute ago they were laughing and joking and now they're silent and watchful.

"You need to keep them in the book," the cashier explains, as if I am not a parent but instead, an infant. "I'm the one who's supposed to tear them out, not you."

I look at the people waiting in line behind me, then down at the loose pieces of paper in my hands. It feels like the walls of this giant superstore are closing in on me. The paper in my hands communicates to the world that I don't have any money. It doesn't help that it is dinnertime, and the store is busy.

I am almost drowning in my humiliation, and yet I'm still aware enough to register how loud the cashier is talking. There can be only one reason for that. This normally anonymous exchange has turned into an angry divide of her against me. And she wants to bolster her ranks by getting the other people in line on her side.

I want to ask her if she has kids. I want to ask her if she is married to their father and if she has ever needed help from anyone and if so, how she felt when she asked for it.

"I don't understand what difference it makes," I say instead, my voice a soft mumble because I am still, against all reason, hoping I can salvage this transaction.

"Well! How do I know you didn't just buy these out in the parking lot? How do I know they're not stolen?"

Oh, now I see. I'm not just a loser. I am a loser and a thief.

"Here you go," I tell the cashier, handing her my food stamps. My voice is not soft anymore but has become a sarcastically jaunty bit of good cheer. "Feel free to check them for fingerprints!"

And with that I take my time smiling at Sam and Randy, I take my time lifting them out of the grocery cart, brushing off the front of their clothes as if this store is so dirty it is beneath our little family's dignity, and then I clasp their tiny hands in mine and together we stroll out of the store and into the sunshine.

Once inside the car, the boys ask me what happened to all our food. I tell them it is all probably still on the conveyor belt, but that I know of a better store, where they sell toys and ice cream instead of meat and vegetables. No argument there, and I drive the two miles from one big box store to another. In my wallet is a credit card for this second store with an unused, $300 limit. The card is my last remaining asset of my tumultuous five-year marriage. And I can think of no better way to put it to good use then by maxing it out on Power Ranger action figures.

In less than an hour, we have another shopping cart and it is not filled to the top but rather holding a few items for discerning shoppers like me. And this time, all three of us are smiling when I reach for my wallet. I pull out the card and the cashier accepts it without a second look. And for just a minute, I am no longer a worthless drain on the system, a woman who couldn't keep a husband happy, a reject, but I am just another shopper indulging her children. No boneless chicken and green beans and vanilla yogurt for us. Our bags are filled with Power Rangers and new superhero shoes with light-up soles and new Spider Man pajamas and a bag of M&M's.

I know running up the balance on my card with toys and

clothes for the boys and a bag of candy for us to share in the car will rank right up there as one of the dumbest things I've ever done. I know I have no way to pay for any of it.

And you know what? It still feels pretty great.

I thought I knew how it would be once I was divorced from my ex, but I was wrong. Even two years later, interactions like the one at the first big box store sap my confidence and remind me how society views single mothers. When the boys were babies and I would take them out in public, they almost always attracted a great deal of attention. People would say things like, "Twins! You and your husband must be so proud." Now I feel like people look at the empty ring finger on my left hand and their faces show only pity.

....

I try not to wallow, but some days, that's harder than others. I suppose my ex is on my mind because the boys are going to be with him for the whole week. I'm getting ready for work and the house is so sadly quiet. I'm lonely. Why couldn't we be happy together?

The only positive thing I can hang onto when I'm missing the boys so much is that, when they are with their dad, I can put all my focus on work. Which I need to do if I want to keep this job. I think the company might be getting ready to downsize, and I don't want them to think they don't need me. I need this job. Maybe I don't want to have it forever, and I know I'm not even very good at it, but right now I need to keep it. And my boss sure has tried to be supportive. He doesn't get mad when I mess up and forget to make the bank deposit, or when my math is off for the payroll. That's the most you can ask for in a boss— understanding—so I'm lucky in that way at least.

This week I have something interesting to look forward to.

I'm going to solve a little mystery. I'm going to find out why so many older people are always coming by the plant asking for something we'd just throw away—gallons of tart cherry juice concentrate.

After cherries get pitted, there's a lot of leftover juice the workers would otherwise be dumping down the drain. It's a pretty dark-red color and looks delicious, but it isn't sweet at all. Nor is it too tart; it is actually just right! Tart cherries are different than sweet cherries. Tart cherries aren't eaten fresh; they're canned and used in baking or dried and used in recipes. So, these people can't be drinking tart-cherry juice straight, can they? And if they were, why would they be doing that? Well, that is what I am about to find out.

Whatever these people are doing with the stuff, I'm going to learn what it is, and why, just to satisfy my own curiosity. And give my brain something to do besides miss my boys, blame my ex for that, and feel sorry for myself.

That day I speak with three different people. Each one is suffering from a different ailment, but all their ailments involve pain. They have something else in common, too. Drinking tart cherry juice works better than anything else to relieve their pain, and they want to talk with me about it. One man excitedly says, "I'm no longer in my wheelchair!" and another man adds, "And I don't need to use my cane anymore to take short walks." He and his wife can dance together again at weddings and anniversary parties, and the pain in her hands that used to keep her from an activity she enjoyed—knitting—is almost gone.

I ask around and oddly, no one here at the plant, nor in the industry as a whole, seems to fully understand how powerful tart cherries are. But soon, I do. Tart cherry juice concentrate relieves arthritis pain and gout. Some people are such regulars at the plant, they've started bringing their own jugs. Within days my mind is bubbling over with ideas. Montmorency tart cherry juice is a natural medicine! People need to know about this. Not just people who live in Leelanau County, and not just people who live in northern Michigan, but everyone, everywhere.

I went to the library and looked it up: Forty million people in the United States suffer from arthritis. Forty million! Montmorency cherry juice can help ease pain. And, farmers here in Leelanau County are the largest producers of Montmorency tart cherries in the world. And yet, because I live here I also know that many of these same farmers are considering selling their orchards to developers because they can't make a living farming. Many farmers are close to retirement age, too, and do not see a way to pass their farms onto their children. Could this be a new, untapped use for these cherries? A vast, new market for our local farmers? Sure, some people were aware of the power of tart cherries. The health benefits had received some national media attention. But as far as I knew, no one was selling tart cherry juice concentrate at grocery stores, not even our local ones. I was so excited to discover this well-hidden secret and wanted to tell the world all about it.

It's all adding up. Take one woman—me—who wants to help people, blend in fresh tart cherry juice from fruit grown on trees by local farmers, stir in people looking for a natural pain remedy, and bam! Something magical is definitely going to happen.

I decide my boss and the plant should bottle the concentrate and sell it in health food stores. They should design a nice label and give this new product a snappy name, like "Miracle Juice," or "Red Razzle." And then they should tell people about it. I'm going to talk to my boss about this. I'm sure the company will jump at the chance to take what they thought was a worthless by-product and make it into something healthy and profitable. Maybe he'll even put me in charge of doing this and give me a raise! The company might be considering downsizing, but this new idea is sure to make me too valuable an employee for them to lose.

When I interviewed for this job of payroll and payable clerk at the plant, I'd never worked in an office before. I was also terrible at math, and I knew nothing about accounting or cherries, and yet my boss still hired me. The interview had gone really well, and I could tell right away that he liked me and liked my optimistic outlook. It is interesting now to remember the one reservation he said he had against hiring me: "You seem too entrepreneurial to stay in this job long term."

At the time I disregarded his comment and told him instead how much I needed the job, and how reliable I'd be. Both things were true, but now I know that Glen's observation also was true. He was right even back then. I took the job because I needed it, but I remember thinking, I am too entrepreneurial to work very much longer for someone else.

My boss wasn't as excited about my new project idea as I was, but in late 1999, he did let me experiment with having some cherry juice concentrate professionally bottled and labeled for retail sale. The plant bottled it from the barrel that workers used to collect the juice. The label said, "Cherry Juice Concentrate," and we had a little logo that said, "Land of Delight." I liked that name. I designed the label with the help of a co-worker and friend, who worked as plant controller. We signed up for a 1-800 phone number and even put together a one-page website. The same people who had been coming by the plant purchased the juice and didn't seem to mind paying for something they used to get for free. We didn't charge much, and it was still less expensive and with fewer side effects than pain pills. Soon we were selling twenty bottles a day of the juice, although sales leveled off. My boss didn't have a marketing budget for "Land of Delight." Not surprisingly, he also didn't give me a raise.

I tried to plead my case about the importance of marketing but to no avail. My thinking was, if nobody knows the benefits of tart cherries except the same people who are getting the concentrate for free, how could it sell? This was obvious to me, but not to anyone else at the plant. I was so intent on the idea, I now worried that my co-workers and my boss thought my outsized enthusiasm had made me a bit nuts.

I accepted that, but what sane single mother could live alone with her twin preschoolers, her good but dead-end job, and her dreams, and not go a little crazy? So, here's what I thought: Crazy is good. Crazy is productive. Crazy is going to help me do something important and valuable.

A week later Bill and I are on a date at the Bluebird, our local tavern. Over the years, this comfortable place has been like a second home to me. I bussed tables here when I was 13, I bartended in between taking college classes toward a degree that I still don't have, and I used it as my escape when my ex and I were fighting and I needed to get out of the house. There are a ton of people here tonight that Bill and I know, and I should be socializing with them. But all I can think about is cherry juice concentrate.

"Can we please talk about something else?" Bill practically begs. "Anything else?"

Obviously, cherry juice is not as interesting to other people, including the man with whom I am in love. But at least he knows that's how I get. I am easily obsessed, and I gravitate to all the energy naturally infused into new ideas. When I'm really interested in something, I find it hard to think about anything else. Even, it seems, when I'm out on a date.

"Okay," I agree. "But just let me tell you this one thing first. Did you know that an eighty-four-year-old woman in Sutton's Bay could now take her dog for a walk again? Did you know a ninety-one-year-old man right here in Leland says he plans to go deer hunting this year for the first time in a long time? And all they did was drink a couple ounces of cherry juice?"

I know I'm talking too fast, and drinking too much, but I also know I couldn't slow my mouth down if I tried. I'm in love with Bill, and I'm also in love with my idea, and this is the first time I've tried to manage both at the same time.

"Did you know all that?" I ask, repeating myself.

"I do now," Bill says, and we both laugh.

His voice sounds resigned, yet tinged with something else, too. Something that sounds almost like, dare I say it, admiration! I really do love this man. He will support my new idea; I just know he will.

All my new idea needs is some good soil to grow in. Even I know that. Northern Michigan soil is fertile, made up of sand, organic matter like leaves and microscopic pieces of bones, as well as grass, rocks, gravel, and silt. The startup soil where I'll be planting my new idea will be fertile, too—a mix of my desire to help people, my work ethic, my belief in this pioneering new business, my daydreams, and a natural red juice with health properties that largely have been undiscovered.

Until now.

LESSON LEARNED

Not everyone will understand your vision no matter how much it may make sense to you.

Roots

2000

I T IS BEFORE DAYLIGHT AND IN MY DREAM, I AM RUNNING. NO MATTER HOW MUCH the terrain changes, my pace remains the same. Up hills, down hills, around corners and taking the curves, I keep my same rhythm. I feel my blood pumping. I feel my lungs inflate, expel the air, and then inflate again. All of this takes almost no effort. My feet connect with the pavement, one at a time, over and over again, yet I do not feel tired. It is sunny, but there is no glare. It is warm, but I am not sweating. There are plenty of other runners, but I don't feel crowded. My shoes feel amazing, almost as if they are magic. I am strong. I am happy. I feel myself smile in my sleep.

Since I started training for the Detroit Marathon, I've had two recurring dreams. The effortless running is the first one; here's the second: I am lost and alone. I know I'm supposed to be running in a long-distance race, but the course is not marked, and when I try various routes, each one leads to a thick forest, a steep drop-off, or an endless swamp I cannot possibly cross on foot. I see people in the distance, but when I try to make my way toward them to ask for help, they disappear, or worse. Sometimes they change into frightening creatures with teeth and claws glinting in some discolored and foreboding sun. I wake up from this dream, exhausted.

"It's an anxiety dream," Bill tells me, adding that dreams like mine are normal and do not mean I'm having unusual emotional difficulties. Especially for someone who got divorced, became a single mother, started a new relationship, wants to quit her job, planned out a new business, trained for a marathon, and returned to college all in just a few short years. Bill studied a lot of human behavior in college and on his job. He's counseled a lot of people; he used to be a probation officer, and now works as a child-welfare consultant. I know he works with people in anxious situations every day, so his words are supposed to comfort me, I'm sure, and yet I find myself wondering something. If my scary running dream is just some inner personal worry looking for a way to come out, is my happy running dream just a mirage? Are all my calm, accomplished feelings made up? Are they just wishful thinking?

I try to work out an answer to this question as I head out to train. I run twenty miles, and by the time I make it back to my driveway, I feel amazing. And I've decided both things are true. The Detroit Marathon will be exciting, and I will feel like I accomplished something real when I complete it. And it will probably be difficult and frightening, and there will be times when I will feel afraid. I've never run a marathon before, so, like Bill says, all of those feelings are normal and can exist side by side. Just like they do in life.

Come to think of it, it's just like parenting my boys by myself. Or, starting a new business. I've never done either of those things before, but I plan to give it my very best and be great at both of them.

Today, of all days, is a day to be positive. To put positive energy out into the world and to share my optimism with the people I love. It's my 35th birthday, and with the exception of that one occasionally recurring running nightmare, it feels wonderful to finally be living this life. I am truly and honestly putting my best forward, in my running and in my life, and it feels great. I have no one to blame for my problems or applaud for my successes. I am responsible for my own actions, and taking that attitude is how I am learning and growing.

....

Sam and Randy are asleep, thank you Lord. They are so excited about starting first grade tomorrow, and I am excited for them. I'm thrilled they are looking forward to school and not dreading it, and even though I will miss our beach days and all the playing outside we do together in the summer, I have adult reasons for being glad it's finally September. With them being in school all day now, my daycare bill will drop to zero, and I'll finally be able to focus on planning this new business. I just know it will be wildly successful.

At the plant, we are selling more cherry juice concentrate every day. I wish I'd be given access to the actual numbers, but my boss is in charge of those. I just know we're still selling to local people, but I'm also boxing it up just about every day to ship to customers beyond our region. Sales have grown little by little, even though my boss hasn't done any marketing or advertising. He lets me sell it, but he doesn't have the enthusiasm for its potential like I do. Actually, no one does.

God put me on this path of coming up with an idea to help so many people, and to make a good life for my family, and I plan to be worthy of that opportunity. I don't see how I can do that by continuing to work for the plant. I need to go off on my own, I'm just not sure how. Especially with two sons to care for and raise.

I just checked on them and could hardly pull myself away from watching them sleep. They are both so innocent and so full of promise and potential. I am amazed at how fast we humans grow. Time is a funny thing. Life without time would probably be amazing. If we all just did what we needed to do, and didn't worry about what time it was, or when this or that would happen, life might have a whole lot more meaning.

I might not know exactly how to go about putting them into action, but I do have big plans. So big in fact that I think they are going to take a lot of time to manifest. In the days ahead, I'll need to try to remember what it felt like to watch my children sleep. I'll need to try to keep from becoming a prisoner of time, someone too busy for what, and for who, are most important to me.

....

I did it! I ran a marathon! It took me five hours and thirteen minutes, but I did it, and even though my lungs still hurt and my legs ache, the whole day felt like something out of a modern-day fairy tale. Except in this one the princess wears running shoes and doesn't give up until the end of the race, even when things get difficult. I've never been a runner, but I trained like one. I've never run a marathon, but I ran one and finished all 26.2 miles! I feel like I can do anything.

Bill, Sam, Randy, and Bill's son, James, and I all drove down to Detroit from Leland the night before the race and stayed with Joyce and Leo, Bill's sister and brother-in-law. I got up early, even before the alarm went off, because I was so nervous. So many thoughts were competing for space in my mind. Did I have what it took to finish? Would I have a time I could be proud of? What would Sam and Randy be doing while I was running?

I ate breakfast, took a shower, and got dressed. Leo drove us to Cobo Hall and dropped us off. Bill and James were running a 5k, Sam and Randy were running a mile-long kid's race, but I was the only one doing the biggie. Excitement made me have to pee, and as soon as Leo dropped us off, I immediately got in line for the bathrooms. The line seemed to go on forever, but I eventually took my turn in the Port-a-Potty, and then went back to check on Sam and Randy and wait with Bill and James. Before I knew it, the race organizers called over a megaphone that all runners needed to get to the starting line. I hugged the boys and James, kissed Bill, and entered the crowd of racers all gathered tightly together.

The starting gun popped, and off I went.

The most surprising thing about the early part of the race was how many people were talking to each other while they were running. I'm a silent runner, so that was weird for me at first. All these people passing me and talking and carrying on while they did it. Then I got used to it, and realized they weren't talking to me, they were talking to themselves, to a friend they were running with, or were just letting me know they were coming up behind on my left or my right.

Here's what I know now about running in a large public marathon that I didn't know before I did it myself: It seems like everyone is passing you because you only see the faster runners who go past; you don't see the ones who started behind you and ended up staying back there for the whole race. Sounds obvious, but in the heat of the moment, it is not.

I calmed my mind and focused on my desire to finish the race, and I tried to forget about what order I might be occupying deep within the thousands of runners. As I ran, the question, "What exactly are you made of?" kept building in my mind. When I was a little girl, and all through my growing-up years, any time I started something and didn't finish it, my parents would try to explain to me the importance of finishing what you started. They meant well, and I probably should have listened to them more, because I often felt like a quitter. In school, I had a lot of ideas for craft projects and school projects, and when I didn't finish them, I had some teachers who called me a quitter. My habit of starting things and not always seeing them through was something my ex-husband reminded me of every chance he got.

"Today is my chance to prove you all wrong," I said out loud.

My stomach grumbled. Race organizers told runners that food would be available for us all along the race course. It would be handed out for free from volunteers whenever we needed a snack. By the seventh mile, I was starving and, lo and behold, there were volunteers handing out sticks of thick, energy-rich fruit puree called "Goo." This was amazing, I thought, grabbing one as I ran by. We didn't even have any package to open; we just had to hold the stick and slurp the nutrition into our mouths.

My subconscious registered something weird, but I dismissed it as just negative energy trying to get into my head. I ate a big ball of Goo off the stick and into my mouth. And I instantly knew I should have listened to my subconscious. Something was not right! That's when I realized other runners were spreading the Goo on their arms and legs and lips . . . they were not eating it! My tongue recoiled, instantly blocking the route down my throat. It wasn't fruit puree the volunteers were handing out; it was Vaseline. Ack! I have a glob of petroleum jelly in my mouth!

What made me think I could do this? I thought. Who do I think I am? I don't even know the difference between edible Goo and Vaseline! But then I remind myself that I am on a mission. My mind is strong and it calms my body.

I quickly stuck both hands into my mouth and scraped as much of the stuff as I could off my teeth and my tongue. Then I followed everyone else's lead. I spread it on my arms and legs and started grabbing proffered cups of water. This was what they'd meant when they said oil and water don't mix. Neither do Vaseline and water.

I managed to get over my humiliation in about a mile, because I couldn't afford the energy to feel it. I had nineteen more miles to go. I actually had a good couple of chuckles to myself over it.

When you can laugh at your mistakes, you can learn from your mistakes.

A few miles later, I caught up with a guy on the Ambassador Bridge, and we ran together for a long time. At about the fifteenth mile, he started taking more and more walking breaks, while I still had the energy to run. He could tell he was slowing me down and told me, firmly, to keep going. I did. I could have used him and the pace he set as an excuse to slow down and walk more, but I didn't. I ran.

By the time the course wound its way onto Belle Isle, I was running by myself with seven or eight of the 26.2-mile route left to go. It became grueling. This section was, by far, the hardest part of the race for me. This was where I found out what I was made of. You know what? I am tough.

After Belle Isle, I ran with a woman named Barbara. She would pass me and then I would pass her, and then we'd switch again until we made it through all the remaining miles together. The .2 of the 26.2 was probably the most mentally challenging experience I had ever had. It doesn't sound like much, but after running twenty-six miles, completing that last bit at a dead run meant a lot. Several joyous minutes later, Barbara and I crossed the finish line together and hugged. What a wonderful, fulfilling experience! Not only am I not a quitter, I am made of some pretty tough stuff. I like who I am. I like what I am, and I feel like I can do anything. Not just with running, but with my life.

After Bill and the boys congratulated me, I made a silent promise to God. One that only He and I know about. I will not waste a single day of what is left of my life. I will use my life for good. I will do something that will help people and help make the world a better place. I have the chance to be a real pioneer in developing a health food no one else has discovered, and I am not going to take that chance for granted. I. Am. Not.

Three weeks later, I was still riding high on Detroit Marathon adrenaline, but even that couldn't keep me excited at work. There is still no one taking my juice idea seriously. Cherry processing is an indstry in northwestern Michigan with a long history. People here call our product "pie cherries" because for decades that is exactly what it has been: Canned cherries to use in cherry pies. A dessert, not a health food. Turning that product 180 degrees is a hard turn for some people here. Well, for most people, it turns out, which continues to frustrate me. A successful, helpful, useful idea is staring us right in the face and no one at the plant sees this but me and one of my co-workers.

I wasn't sure if they didn't believe tart cherry juice had medicinal properties, if they thought all the older people who swore by it were just imagining things, or if my co-workers just didn't want to do the work it took to develop a new product. It was very difficult to see an opportunity, to share the idea of that opportunity, with people who had the tools to take advantage of it, and to watch them do nothing.

I had no idea what was coming, but this would be just the first sign of the difficulties I would encounter working in a traditional, and yes, male-dominated, industry. Most of the people with authority at the plant are men. And they have decided I know enough to sell the product, but not enough to put a real plan in place to make juice sales a part of the plant's business. I'm not sure if it is because I am a woman or because I have such a new idea. Probably a little of both.

· ·

I've had some good success. Our bottled concentrate is now for sale at a local food co-op. But it has been weeks since I made that contact, and instead of giving me time to investigate how we can get tart cherry juice concentrate into retail stores all around the country, my boss sent me to a conference on safety procedures for food manufacturers. The safety class wasn't for bottling, and it wasn't for developing new agricultural products, it was for the plant as a whole. Someone needed to go and I guess I was the one who could be spared from her work.

I didn't mind going on the road for work. It's just that I would have preferred to be visiting retail stores and trade shows and demonstrating our juice, not donning plastic glasses and learning about plant safety.

I was on the road by 8 a.m. With some effort, I accepted this assignment and was determined to go back to the office confident in what I learned. I certainly didn't want the company's pie filling or bottled cherry juice to give anyone food poisoning, or for anyone in the plant's administration office to be fined for negligence. I felt like I was gaining my boss's respect if he trusted me with this responsibility, and yet what I really wanted to do was sell tart cherry juice concentrate on my own, in my own way, and be compensated well for it.

I had been asking for a raise for more than a month, and the answer was always the same: There was no money in the budget to pay me more. Every week, we'd sell more juice. I still didn't know how much. No one shared numbers with me on what was my idea, but each week I was shipping more and more. I wished they'd give me a raise. I wasn't asking for the company to spend money they didn't have in order to pay me more. I was asking for a three-percent commission to go on the road and sell cherry juice concentrate.

All of this was on my mind as I learned about safety techniques I could take back to share with the plant. By 3 p.m., the conference was over, and although I wanted to daydream about my new ideas, I had focused on what I was there for and my job. I learned about a number of safety precautions the plant could have been taking that we were not, and communicating these to everyone and making them happen was going to be enough work for two full-time people. Between my regular job in payroll and payables, trying to grow the tart cherry juice concentrate bottling project, and now being tasked with company safety, I was going to be extra busy.

I was also learning more every day, and my resume was getting stronger. I knew they'd said no before, but I approached my boss again. I had done well as a payroll and payable clerk, I told him. I saw a new opportunity and helped market a new product "made to sell". It was selling. I attended the safety conference and brought back ideas the plant could use. Now, can I go on the road, sell our bottled tart cherry juice concentrate, and be paid a three-percent commission for my work? I was denied.

Hitting that obstacle to my idea was hard, and I didn't think anything could take my mind off starting my own business. Turned out, I was wrong. There was one thing that could: A big fat engagement ring!

Bill proposed to me, right in my living room.

"Okay," he said, looking into my eyes with purpose and strength, "this is the deal."

He'd already asked Sam and Randy for their blessing, and I'd watched while they nodded their heads like crazy—"Yeah, yeah, super-duper yeah!" Then he actually recited a beautiful poem he'd written for me a long time ago, and then he asked me to marry him.

"Yes, yes, yes, all over the place, yes!" I told him.

Bill slid a ring with a lovely and sparkling purple Tanzanite rock onto my finger. I had no idea Bill had already asked my dad for permission to marry me. What I did know was that together, he and I had the power to make our lives go any way we wanted.

With a unified effort, a lot of attitude, gratitude, and desire, we could and would be great together. We could and would be great with our children. We could and would love each other as God loved us, and we could and would project the love inside of us onto our family, and then outward and into everything we do.

Bill will be a wonderful influence on my sons, but he has also been a devoted father to his children from his first marriage, James and Jessica. They are both older, James is 17 and Jessica is 20, and although we don't see Jessica often, Bill cares deeply for both of them. My soon-to-be husband was a friend to everyone he meets, a wise man people go to for advice, and Bill had become my rock. He is a lover, a poet, a counselor, and in every way I know of, a good and decent man. And soon, he would be my husband and Sam and Randy's stepfather.

SIDE NOTE

Productivity and drive was not my weakness! Standing up for what was right was!

When I am feeling anxious, worried, or down, I remember a line from the wedding poem Bill wrote for me: Unconditional, she said to me, that's how my love would have to be.

Sapling

2001 - 2003

VERY SLOWLY, THE BOYS AND I ARE MOVING OUR BELONGINGS INTO BILL'S PLACE. It is a classic two-story northern Michigan house, with Cape Cod architecture and gray shingles. It sits on a friendly neighborhood corner in downtown Leland. Bill's grandfather built the house in 1952, and it has been in the White family ever since, so Bill knows everyone in town and everyone knows him. Sometimes it feels like everyone knows our business, but mostly I just chalk that up to living in a small town, where this tends to be true anyway. I'm going to make a point of not letting that bother me. I'm going to concentrate on my relationship with Bill instead of worrying so much about what other people think.

Years ago, my parents bought a unique piece of property on a land contract. They were able to turn one of the buildings into a modest four-hundred-square-foot house—we called it "the guest house." And since my split from my ex in 1996, Sam, Randy and I had been living in this rental just north of town. Even though our place was tiny, with barely space to turn around in, my parents' house and outbuildings are on several acres, so I was used to having more privacy. Moving into Bill's is going well, but sometimes I miss the open spaces of my parents' land. They are only three miles away, but that does not make me miss their familiar property any less. With that in mind, here's what I know on this cold January day at the start of my 36th year on this planet: The more we humans do, the more we humans get, the more we humans want.

I certainly include myself in that generalization, me and my daydreams and my desires. For proof, I'd just have to look inward and consider my current state of mind. I'm adjusting to being a single mom, but I want to get married. I have a service-able job, but I have entrepreneur blood—both my grandfathers and my father were entrepreneurs—and I want to start my own business. I make ends meet (barely), but I want to make a good living so that I can make a difference in this world. I continually question my faith and my spiritual purpose, knowing how ethe-real such feelings are, and yet I want concrete answers.

When I take stock of my life, I know some of these wants are ongoing, and some are finite. Bill and I have set a wedding date, so satisfying my want to be married is on its way to happening, and I could not be more thrilled about it. I am more in love with Bill every day. He's been taking me with him to church, and because of that I've been reading the Bible. So, my spiritual curiosity is being awakened. Often, I will read the same verse over and over again, trying to understand its meaning and its application to my daily life. Once I relax, and force my mind to be still and quiet, the beginnings of understanding often come. I believe it is only when I am quiet that God tells me what I need to know.

I realize my need for spiritual fulfillment is a process, one I've started and one I plan to stick with. So, for the time being, I feel like I am doing the things necessary to satisfy that want. In order for us to be married at St. Paul's and by their pastor, I have to take a class. And, there is a confirmation class beginning in the spring, and I might just sign up for that, too.

My wedding plans and my spiritual plans are the good news. But my other want—to be rewarded for my big idea to help people and make money from a by-product at work—is going nowhere.

In retrospect, it's obvious to me that I was the one who ran with the cherry concentrate idea at the plant, and that even though he didn't say this out loud, it feels like all my efforts went against my boss's wishes. Otherwise, even though I can tell that sales are increasing just by how many boxes I'm shipping, I have not been compensated for coming up with the idea. Or for working to make it profitable. How profitable I don't know because that information isn't shared, but it must be because the plant is now selling a product they used to either throw away or give away for free.

I promised myself I would ask again for a commission raise, but I never did. I know what the answer would be and this more than anything has me thinking constantly about going out on my own. The plant hasn't compensated me financially, but I haven't been compensated emotionally, either. Not even so much as a "Good job!" from my bosses. I'll admit, that bothers me. The plant could be selling juice like crazy if my boss would just put a little energy and resources behind it. I had no way of knowing this at the time, but this same issue would follow me even after I left the plant. It would come up again and again with the investors.

Of all my current wants, starting my own business is the one I think is in my control to satisfy. There, I've said it. I want to quit my job and start selling cherry concentrate on my own. I would have already done that by now if I weren't so scared of failing. And, in order to do it I will have to quit. I don't have any other choice, because I'll be in direct competition with my employer, and I know that would never fly.

But quitting is terrifying! I have my boys to think about, and I can't expect Bill to provide for all three of us. His kids are now adults and out of the house and living independently, but he still has household bills of his own to pay. I know I need to bring in money, too, but I'm not being paid what I'm worth at the plant. All I want is to go on the road and sell concentrate for an extra three-percent commission. Twice I've asked for this and twice been refused. To this day, I'm not sure why I try to see this from my boss's perspective, but I can't. Yes, they'd be paying me more, but they'd be making more than enough to make up for it.

It's a conundrum. I don't know if I should try to get a better-paying job somewhere else and give up on starting my own company, or if I should just take a chance and go for it. I feel so compelled to start my own business to help people and to save farms from development that I don't think I'm going to be able to stop myself even if I wanted to. Which, I don't. Northern Michigan survives on agriculture and tourism, and there aren't many jobs available that pay well. I don't know if I can get a better-paying job than the one I currently have, no matter how hard I try. Plus, the thought of starting my own juice concentrate company is so very exciting!

> **LESSON LEARNED**
>
> **Make sure you have another source of revenue before starting a business. Lack of capital is a number one reason to fail. And a founder's salary only begins when there's money for everything else.**

I can almost picture it. It would be called, "Leland Cherry Company," and it would produce healthful tart cherry juice concentrate that would be sold in stores across the United States. Maybe even internationally! I love selling cherry juice concentrate to people. I love to see them smile. I love thinking that something I do could improve people's health and let them live a more pain-free life. In that way, a juice company would fulfill my career wants, and my spiritual wants, and what could be better than that.

I pray to God this night to please give me an answer in my sleep.

Should I be bold? Or should I play it safe?

There was a time when I hated hearing people tell me: "The Lord works in mysterious ways." If I was confused about something and asked for advice or a shoulder to lean on, and someone responded with that annoying saying, all it did was make me roll my eyes and totally shut down.

I've struggled with my faith for a long time, and I used to blame God for the bad things that happened to me and to the world. If God was so full of grace, I wondered, then why wasn't the world a better place?

Now I know it is we humans who cause all the problems, not God. And, while I still think there are more original ways to say that God has a plan that we mortals might not understand, I have to admit, there is a mysterious component to life we should embrace. I mean, how could I have known that my question about starting my own business was ultimately going to be answered by two people I never even thought of, and yet who I've known my whole life? How could I know that some of the best advice I'd ever get would come in the form of a question from my sons when they were still little? Back then I remember driving somewhere, the boys were in the backseat and I had so many ideas in my head they couldn't help but spill from my mouth. Meaning, I was talking to myself out loud. When Sam piped up in his six-year-old voice and said, "Mom, if you could choose what you would do, what would you choose?" It struck me as such a wise question, and of course I knew the answer. I'd start my own business helping people by selling them cherry juice concentrate.

The answer to how I would do this arrived in the form of my parents. A father who has a lifetime of business experience, a great big personality, and a zest for life that is unparalleled. And a mother who supports almost everything I do, good, bad, or indifferent.

LESSON LEARNED

Quitting a job to start a business rarely works. Keep working and start your business on the side. Quit your job once the business is profitable.

Scientific studies have shown that an only-child has an advantage in business. They tend to be more entrepreneurial than children raised with siblings. The theory behind these studies is that an only-child, who misses out on sibling rivalries, isn't driven to conform to any particular family role and might feel freer to develop whatever natural aptitudes she or he are born with. Without sisters or brothers, an only-child becomes used to the presence of adults from the get go, and often develops her or his verbal and interpersonal skills while still very young.

I am an only-child, but I didn't know about any of that research while I was starting my business. I only knew I felt driven to be financially and personally successful, and to make a difference in the world, and that I was never going to achieve any of that by working as a payroll clerk in a cherry processing plant.

"Michelle, I think you might be onto something," my dad tells me one evening.

My dad has had high expectations of me ever since I was a little girl, and he has them still. This is the first time in a long time I've felt like he's taking me seriously about something that matters to me, and my chest swells with pride.

"I know I'm onto something," I tell him, and then I start talking as fast as I can get the words out.

Does he know that hundreds of people come to the plant for cherry juice concentrate every week and swear by the results they get from drinking it? Does he know the plant managers used to consider this juice a problematic by-product, but that I strongly believe it is now being sold at a good profit? Does he know that no one else in our whole region is capitalizing on this business niche, even though we are surrounded by thousands of acres of cherry orchards? Does he know that there is not enough demand for cherries, sales of canned pie filling are on the decline, and farmers are starting to switch to grapes or hops, or even sell their farms, and that could mean over-development for our beautiful county? I so wanted my boys to experience the same local beauty that I did as a kid. It defined my childhood, and I cannot imagine them growing up without the rolling hills and orchards of Leelanau County. I didn't see condos everywhere, and I don't want them to, either.

If my dad didn't know all of this before we sat down to talk, he does now. And, he must share these same feelings, because he suggests that he and I go into business together. The deal is this: He'll write a business plan and seek out bank loans and investors, in exchange for forty percent of the company. I'll own the other sixty percent and be responsible for setting up an office and establishing relationships with suppliers so that we can start production and begin packaging and marketing the juice concentrate to wholesalers and retailers. We did all this together, while Bill and my mom cheered us on.

> **LESSON LEARNED**
> **What to look for in a mentor - how does it change if the mentor is also an investor - or a relative? Or both?**

I say yes! And, I already know how I'm going to accomplish my part of the set-up responsibilities: trade shows. Once buyers hear my story about the processing plant, and I tell them about all the older people buying cherry juice concentrate to help their arthritis, I bet they'll be climbing over each other to place orders.

My dad and I shake on our agreement, just like real business partners, and on the kitchen table in my parents' house, the Leland Cherry Company is born.

I give notice at the plant because I can't keep working there and start a competing business. It wouldn't be ethical and I don't have the time. My first day as a businesswoman I spend vacillating between feeling excited and feeling anxious. There's so much to gain, but there is also so much to do.

My dad and I need an office, we need desks and computers and filing cabinets. We need a website. We need a logo and stationery and business cards. We need a supplier of cherry juice concentrate, and a bottle design, and labels, and retail accounts. And, at least until my dad gets some investors, we need to finance this start-up ourselves. Conventional wisdom says you should build your business first, and then approach investors when you are ready to grow. I didn't know that when my dad and I started Leland Cherry Company, and I'm not sure my dad did either. We were both entrepreneurial in nature, but neither of us had ever built a health food company from scratch.

I gave myself the promotion the plant refused to give me, but I no longer had a paycheck. We needed money.

....

I am now the president and CEO of Leland Cherry Company, and I am raring to go. Look out world, tart cherry juice concentrate is about to take you by storm. The healthy properties of cherries are coming soon to a grocery store, health food store, and big box store near you!

Hundreds, even thousands of bottles of bright red juice concentrate will be stacked on store shelves. Just as soon as my dad and I figure out where the capital to get us started will come from.

Tonight, I'm going to pray again, this time for funding to get our business up and running. When I needed an answer about what I should do about my job, God wasted no time in pointing me toward my dad. There's no one I trust more, and now my new company will benefit from his business experience, his wisdom, and his outsized personality. I'm a little bit worried about being overwhelmed by his big personality and his socializing, but

that's the daughter in me, not the businesswoman. He's a professional, I know that, and we are going to be great together.

We have each other. I am working on setting up our office
and contacting potential retail customers and my dad is almost
finished with the business plan. What we need now is money.

And I can hardly wait to see how God provides it for us.

• •

Sleep will not come. I try not to toss
and turn, because Bill is lying next to
me, and I don't want to wake him up.
But lying still feels like torture. Bursts
of anxiety start to pulse through my
arms and my legs, making the urge
to thrash and flounder almost overwhelming. I can't get comfortable.
The sheets feel like restraints, and I
sweat under my imagined captivity.

> ## LESSON LEARNED
> So you've got an idea
> for a business. Start
> small, work from home,
> in your spare time until
> you start to approach
> profitability.

What if I can't pay my bills? What if I don't have enough
money to buy school clothes for Sam and Randy? What if I fail
and Bill loses respect for me?

It's been two months since we became an official business, and
yet my dad has not been able to get a single investor interested
in our company. The banks won't give us so much as a small
commercial loan without collateral, and I don't have any. My
parents' house is already over-mortgaged, so using that won't
work. I thought it was only my boss at the plant who refused to
understand the value of tart cherry juice concentrate, but I was
wrong. It's hard to get anyone to understand, bankers and investors included. The people who do understand it are the people
who are using it every day, but those are not the people with
money to lend or invest.

I tiptoe out of bed, shutting the bedroom door behind me.

Sam and Randy are with their dad this week, so instead of checking on them I walk to the front window and look out at our peaceful little neighborhood. Leland is so quiet and calm, it looks like midnight in a Norman Rockwell illustration. And yet inside my body a dark wave of worry rages.

I pray a silent prayer that this company will provide a living for me and for my family, and for my parents. Success to me is not major wealth, but if tart cherry juice concentrate is healing and reviving and we make money by selling it to people who need it, then I will have succeeded because I will be helping people.

> **LESSON LEARNED**
>
> Financing a new business with credit cards is never a good idea. The money isn't free! It all has to be paid back and 0% doesn't last long.

I walk back to our bedroom and open my dresser drawer as quietly as I can so as not to wake Bill. I take out the pre-approved credit card applications that regularly find their way into our mailbox. While banks have been stingy, credit-card companies seem to be giving money to anyone, even people who quit their job to start a business. In the past, I've always torn these offers up and burned them in the fireplace or thrown them away. Two weeks ago, we applied to a third bank for a loan, adding information to our business plan about non-traditional markets like marathon runners and truck drivers, to no avail. After the third bank turned down our loan application, I started saving those credit card mailings.

I go back out into the kitchen and sit down at the table, take out a pen, fill out all the applications, and seal the envelopes. A loan is a loan is a loan. What does it matter if the money comes from a local bank, or an investor, or a credit card company? At an introductory zero percent interest, there is no way I can go wrong, right? I know the Leland Cherry Company is going to be so successful.

I put the envelopes in the stack of outgoing mail and go back to bed. Tomorrow I will take them to the post office. I know it took me a long time, but I must have finally gone back to sleep because the next time I open my eyes, the sun is out, and Bill has already left for work. I get dressed and head straight to the post office and put the envelopes inside the mail slot and feel so excited.

Driving back home, I feel two more things: One, in order to have our business take off, I had to do that, and two, now that I have there's no turning back.

• •

One warm day in March I walk again to the mailbox, this time to get the mail, not to mail something, and there they are. Our incorporation papers! The Leland Cherry Company has existed in my mind for almost a year, but now it exists in real life. Plus, MasterCard and Visa obviously think more highly of me than any local bank does. As a matter of fact, they think highly enough to extend me $35,000 in credit. At the time, this made me feel like a real businesswoman with a real business. What I know now is, if your business plan states it will take one year to be profitable, add another two years to that. If you think you need $35,000, triple it. There are so many unknown factors that will require money and you cannot possibly prepare for all of them. Little did I know going into this how much debt I would incur. That $35,000 is enough to rent a small office and retail space in Leland, enough to get a website built, set up agreements to buy cherry concentrate from local processors, decide to use a distinctive bottle design my dad found and arrange for it to

> **LESSON LEARNED**
> The only way to plan for the unknown is to double the amount of time you think you'll need to be profitable and triple the amount of start-up cash.

be manufactured for us, buy a van and pay for travel to trade shows, and "hire" our first employee, Craig Smith.

I say "hire" but he won't take any money. As a friend of my dad's, he actually wants to work for free, which I cannot understand but don't argue with. Craig, or "Smitty," as he was called, has a lot going for him. He is the son of a cherry farmer, so he understands the motives behind our new business. He's also a retired colonel so leadership ability is a given and I feel like God sent him to us. He constantly encourages me, and his encouragement is often presented like a military salute, which makes me feel both proud and filled with responsibility. I look forward to using his wisdom and discipline to make the company succeed.

"Young lady," Smitty says, whenever I am feeling overwhelmed, "there are never problems, only opportunities."

I vow to make his attitude my attitude. Some days, it even works.

I began taking substitute-teaching jobs, and in hindsight I should have taken more of them, but my days were so full already. I'm busy making my sons' school lunches, trying to keep up on the laundry that two seven-year-old twin boys generate, helping to plan their sports banquets, taking them to their little league games and cheering them on, plus being a soon-to-be wife and a full-time mother. While the boys are with me 40% of the time, I still think about, plan activities for, and love them 100% of the time. I try to find time to sleep, but it is not easy. In a year's time, I graduated from college with a BA in Family Life Education, completed Lutheran confirmation, gotten engaged, and started Leland Cherry Company. But I cannot stop to think on all this. I have to just keep going.

This month, Sam and Randy will turn seven, and I can hardly believe it. It seems like just a few minutes ago, they were toddlers. I am so excited about my new company and our product that I just want to tell everyone about it. There isn't much that can tear me away from work these days, but a birthday party for my twins is one thing that can. I might not have much in terms of wealth or possessions, but I can give the boys a day they'll remember.

And, I do! Sam and Randy invite all their friends, and we play games and eat cake at Hancock Field, a little park right up the road. It is an unseasonably warm day, as if God is giving my twins a little sun for their special day. Just not too hot to melt the ice cream! As I watch the boys sit at the picnic table with their friends, and laugh and roughhouse, I can't help but let my thoughts drift to the business. I need to figure out our logo and the rest of our graphics so they all look unified. I need to make this business a success for them, so that we can build a more stable life.

• •

I love my little office. Unlocking the door every morning, turning on the lights, and sitting down at my desk makes me feel so good. We got a great deal on two small shed-like buildings near the harbor in Leland, the historic district, that are perched right on the edge of Lake Michigan. Ironically, this is near where my parents had a family restaurant at one time. My parents had even once owned this very building on the corner of Lake and Pearl Streets. They had sold it and then I rented from the new owner and then, later, purchased it.

Turning on my laptop makes me feel like I have accomplished something, even though I know I will accomplish so much more in the

> **LESSON LEARNED**
> Little did I know how much time I would miss with my children by deciding to start a business. The business became my top priority and even when I was with my boys, I was thinking about work.

future. Here is how I see it: By the time Sam and Randy are teenagers, our lives will be perfect. Bill and I will be several years into our happy marriage, and my business will be debt-free and thriving. I will be the entrepreneur I always hoped to be, and Leland Cherry Company will be financially successful beyond my wildest dreams. Bill and I and the boys will be able to afford to travel the world together. My mom, the consummate cheerleader, mediator, and promoter will be happy for us, and my dad and I will have an unbreakable bond, even tighter than the one we have now. My parents' financial health will be assured as they grow older and prepare to retire. Because of the company and our hard work to build it, hundreds of thousands, if not millions, of people will have been helped by the healing properties of tart cherry juice concentrate. Maybe I will even have discovered new uses for this amazing fruit, which will bring even more business to local farmers. They will be able to keep farming, and to pass their farms onto their children instead of selling out to developers.

When I let myself imagine such a big future for us, the familiar voices of my schoolteachers and my parents soon bring me back to Earth. "Get your head out of the clouds, Michelle," I hear them say. "Stop living in a dream world."

Except I have my own company now, and those voices don't sound quite so critical to me anymore. Instead, they've started to sound almost practical. That's because every day there is something—okay, many somethings—for me to do that I know will bring me one step closer to my dream. Today that something is planning our travel to the Flying Pig Marathon in Cincinnati, Ohio.

....

To get the company up and running as soon as possible, my dad and I made an agreement with a local cherry farming operation,

Amon Orchards, to bottle our cherry juice concentrate. It's spring and we sell our juice at local farm markets and we've even received a few phone and website orders. We haven't sold much yet, and definitely not as much as I'd like, but we are starting to pick up local

accounts and I think we are beginning to get a following. The plant where I used to work is still selling cherry juice concentrate. And, as far as I can tell, still not doing any marketing. I feel excited because I am going to be able to do all the things in my own business that I wanted to do for them.

My dad is a master at brainstorming non-traditional markets, and weeks ago he, Bill, Craig, and I decided people you wouldn't think of, like marathon runners and truck drivers, are a great market for our concentrate. I'd tried explaining this to the banks that turned down our loans, but they wouldn't listen and even advised me not to reach out to these markets. They're health-conscious, I said, they have aches and pains, they have disposable income to spend on new products, and they are numerous and easily reachable. Being a marathoner myself, I know they'll also be in pain, and cherry juice concentrate is a good pain reliever.

My dad and I decide to employ a time-tested business sales strategy: divide and conquer. Bill and I will cover the marathon in Cincinnati, while my dad heads east with a friend to showcase our new product at a trucker show. Someone has to stay home with my mom and keep the office running, so Smitty said he was the one for that. I never realized how many details and how much organizing this new business would require, but we are managing.

The practical side of highlighting our concentrate at the Flying Pig is that we'll have zero competition. Bill and I will be handing out samples to runners at the pre-race Marathon Expo, and then selling bottled juice at the race. Other juice companies would never in a million years think of investigating this new market. It's brilliant!

Or, at least that's what we thought at the time. What we didn't take into consideration was that most runners do not want to try something new just before a race. Not even a taste. And since no one knew about the health benefits of tart cherries yet, it was an educational show for us, not a selling show. We spent hours attempting to tell people about the benefits of tart cherries and ran into—quite literally—a great deal of skepticism.

But back then we were pumped and ready. Marathon day arrives, and I'm excited, nervous, and feel all kinds of other emotions I have no words for. I remember how I felt as a runner, and feel the adrenaline surge through my body again, even though this time, I'm a vendor and not a runner. I'm anxious to be at the starting line with all the hustle and bustle; anxious to debut our juice to just the people who can surely benefit from it.

Together Bill and I make the eight-hour drive safely to Cincinnati with a rented U-Haul full of tart cherry juice concentrate made from northern Michigan cherries. This is precious cargo—it takes eighty cherries to make a single ounce of juice. We don't have our company bottles yet, so we worked with a local farm whose owners had jumped on the idea of the health benefits of cherries while I was still at the processing plant. They thought the same way I did, and I was sure this early partnership would work out well. They offered to pack the juice into quart-sized mason jars. If anyone opened the back of our U-Haul, they might have thought we were bootleggers!

"What are the directions to the race?" Bill asks me as we reach Cincinnati.

He's driving, and although he didn't need a map to get to Cincinnati from Michigan, since our route was all on main interstates, now that we're getting close to the city, and traffic is heavy, he needs directions. He wants to know which exit to take, where to park, and what part of the city the marathon is in. And I have no idea what to tell him. I was so busy getting ready for the race I didn't think to get directions to the race. How am I ever going to run a business if I can't even get us to our first sales event?

"Um, well . . ." I hedge, trying to think of something, but Bill sees through me and his shoulders slump.

"You don't know where we're going, do you?" he asks, annoyed.

"Nope," I admit. "But I think it's over there. Take this exit and then take a right."

I have no idea why I think that. I have no idea why I say it to Bill, but since it sounds like as good a plan as any, Bill takes the exit, takes a right, and then another right, and suddenly there we are, at the parking lot reserved for vendors like us. Bill turns off the engine and looks at me with a combination of mystification and admiration. Maybe I can do this business thing after all.

"What can I say?" I tell Bill, my confident tone returning with gusto. "I guess the universe agrees with us, and we're supposed to be here."

· ·

In the days and months and years to come, I will learn that just because the universe agrees with you, that doesn't mean the universe feels any compunction to make things easy. At that marathon, Bill and I gave out hundreds and hundreds of samples of cherry juice concentrate to all the runners who came to pick up their packets the day before the race. We told them how much it would help. Most ignored us and just kept going. Interestingly, it was the kids who were best for pulling in a sale. They knew a good thing when they saw it! As I handed out samples and extolled the virtues of tart cherries, my hope was that the next day they would notice less pain because of the cherry juice.

We sold three bottles of concentrate. Three. Twenty thousand runners, and we were only able to get three of them to buy a bottle of our juice concentrate. To say I was over optimistic with my sales projections when we planned this trip is putting it mildly.

After I'm home for a few days, I reassess. Sales-wise, the trip was a bust and a waste of money. However, we did meet some people who might turn out to be solid contacts for wholesale leads. And Bill and I learned we could work an event together. That part of the plan went so smoothly, it was like we'd worked with each other for years.

But now I need to take a good look at myself and my plans for this new business. I had great expectations for this trip. I would not listen to the bankers or anyone else who tried to give me advice. The trip had been expensive and had a low return. I know we had to get the word out somehow, but this was not the way. I was determined to make my product a household brand. I accepted the fact that to do so I was going to have to throw a lot of spaghetti at the walls to find a market that would stick. For now, I had to decide what to do with the product that didn't sell at the Flying Pig. There was no way I could know this then, but later on the Detroit Free Press Marathon would turn out to be one of our best-selling avenues. We'd been on to something even with the Flying Pig; we just needed to wait for the general public to catch on.

If I go to the farm (our supplier) and pay to have them re-label our quarts with their label, I won't be stuck with a big bill for something I didn't sell. The trip did cost me money, and a ton of my precious pride, too. Amon Orchards graciously took the product back and re-labeled what we did not need and used them for their farm market. Although we hired them to do our bottling, they were also a competitor of sorts. They only sold the concentrate from their own farm market and we sold our concentrate everywhere else, but they were making sales that we were not. I was still grateful for their help, and glad to provide a little revenue for them. Dave Amon was the first person I'd met who was as passionate about tart cherry concentrate as I was.

....

The trip was fun, but failure is not. My credit card payments are all due. No interest, because we're still in the grace period, but that will come soon enough. We just got this business started, and I can't believe we fell this far behind so fast. It feels like the beginning of the marathon I ran, when all the other racers were passing me, and I felt like I wasn't up for the challenge. Like I couldn't keep up. Like I was being swept along and at any moment I might fall down. Except with a business, other people are depending on me to keep it going. If I fall down, I won't just skin my knee or scrape my palms, I'll take my family down with me.

There are, however, some feelings of hope at this hard time. I'm still excited about being able to make something that helps people, I'm going to church with Bill, and unlike at some other times in my life, I feel like I'm handling stress reasonably well. Back when my ex and I were having problems, I often drank too much to relieve my anxiety. The problems and worry with the business are equally stressful, and yet I'm not automatically turning to alcohol. Life is still complicated, I still have challenges to face, but at least I'm not self-medicating.

....

One thing that helps is going to church with Bill. I thought this would just help my spiritual self, but it helps my work self too. That's because they are connected, and trying to separate them no longer makes sense to me. I am determined not to be one person on Sunday and someone else the rest of the week. I am one woman: mother, wife, business striver and faithful believer all seven days. Or that is my goal, anyway. In retrospect, I was just willing myself to believe. My faith then was new. And small.

Just like starting my business made me feel like I was doing what I was supposed to do with my life, going to church makes me feel like I belong while living my life. That's what I'm going to say to anyone who asks why I joined a church. Why I couldn't just go there, why I felt compelled to become a member. I'll tell them it feels like I belong not just to this local group of worshippers at this local church, but that I belong at this time, in this place, in this world. That's so important to me. I guess I didn't realize how important until now.

Today I was confirmed as an official member of St. Paul's church. And it feels wonderful! Like I am a part of something huge and glorious and part of my overall life becoming whole. I have something to work toward—business success—and something to live within—my faith. When I worked at the plant, those two things would have seemed so separate. Now that I am working to build my own company, they don't seem separate at all.

Bill helped make the day special and helped me feel special inside, too. First, he took me downtown and we went shopping for a new dress. I can't remember the last time I bought a dress, and I love what I chose: A black and white pattern that I think looks modern but also virtuous. This morning as I was getting ready, Bill presented me with a corsage for the ceremony, and he'd already arranged for the altar flowers to be in honor of me. He even ordered a special cake for us to have afterwards at a little reception. At the time, I thought I'd finally achieved a meaningful relationship with God. I thought joining a church made that happen. Now I know it was only the beginning of that relationship.

I'd struggled with my work life for so many years, but I'd

struggled with my faith for just as long, if not longer. I couldn't even say the words "my faith" because I didn't have any. I thought the Bible was written by a bunch of hypocrites who interpreted the book their way just to convince people to think like they did. I thought that if there were a God, surely this world would be a better place. Now I know that bad things happen, because people are fallible. God gave us free will; sometimes we use that gift well and sometimes we don't. My sons are with their dad, but standing at church with Bill and James by my side, I pledge that after today, I'm going to try harder to do more of the former and less of the latter. When things at the company get scary and I start to worry, I'll pray instead, and know that God will take care of me—of us—in his way.

> **LESSON LEARNED**
> Your business life is not separate from your faith journey. It is all part of a whole. Your business should fit in with your faith and your ethics.

Days pass and I work harder than ever. The business is making small strides while at the same time, dealing with big issues. Most of these revolve around money—what else—but my dad and I are also learning to work with each other. Sometimes I forget that he is my business partner and not just my dad. A lot of times he forgets that I own sixty percent of the company and am not just his daughter. I continue to be optimistic that we will work these things out. What are the right words to address this with him? I am trying so hard to figure that out.

I'm also taking stock of my life, since my wedding day is drawing close. Now that I feel more balanced and am learning to deal better with stress, and now that I'm going to church, and in a healthy relationship, and being a better mother to the boys, the mistakes I've made in my past seem incomprehensible to me. How could I have spent so much time under the control of alcohol? Now that I am free of it, I see all the damage it did to me, to my sons, and to my first marriage. Now that I am free of it, I also see the damage it can still do to people I am close to and care about. I wish anyone who feels under its control could experience the peace I feel. This was the first time I gave alcohol a break. There would be others.

I can only do what I can do, and I've decided to concentrate on building a successful business and pray that this will be a golden opportunity for me and for my family. That it will give purpose and financial security to me, to Bill, to our children and to my parents. Success to me is having time with my family, being financially stable, and fulfilling my dreams of helping other people. If tart cherry juice concentrate is healing and reviving, and we make money with it, then I will have succeeded, because I will be helping people and saving farms, which in turn will preserve this beautiful county. Being able to help people who I love, and people I will never meet, feels so powerful.

....

Today's the day! Today's the day to look my past in the eye and say goodbye to it. Goodbye to the hurt, goodbye to the failures, goodbye to the anxiety and the self-doubt. Today I am going to marry my best friend. All the love Bill and I share, all our dreams for the future, and our desire to be a family together will be sealed up tight in one soul this afternoon. All the family on Bill's side is here, and I know that as I grow within myself I am much better prepared to be a great wife and mother. Family is so important, and Bill and I are about to create a family that is filled with love and devotion.

The Old Art Building in Leland looks magical when I arrive. I am still getting to know Bill's family, but I've already picked up on the fact that Bill's sister, Joyce, and Bill's sister-in-law, Joyce, are very different from each other and may not see eye to eye. And yet, it thrills me to see they've worked together perfectly to give us a dream wedding. I call Bill's sister "Joyce Marlene," and his sister-in-law "Joyce Elaine," so I can keep up with who is who. Two months ago, the Joyce's asked me what details I wanted for my wedding. I've been so overwhelmed with work, school, church, and the boys and Bill, that all I could think of were my two favorite colors. "Purple and sage," I blurted out. "Can you do something with that?"

The two Joyce's took it from there. They made all the food. They tied ribbons on everything. They hung a beautiful antique chandelier outside from a tree branch and set up all the chairs. They made the Old Art Building (now it is called the "Leelanau Cultural Center"), and the grounds look so lovely for our ceremony and for the reception afterwards that when I first arrive, I am speechless. I'd spent the day at the beach with Sam and Randy while everyone else prepared our special day.

The weather is cooperating, so we hold the ceremony outside. My dad walks me down the aisle while my mom watches lovingly from the side. I look into my dad's face and think about how important he has been, and will always be, in my life. He's so proud . . . he looks like the Cheshire cat. Then I look over at my mom and the boys, and my life feels so full and yet, full of peace, too.

When I get to the altar and see Bill standing so straight and strong and waiting for me, I can't help it, I start to bawl. I'm not even sure why, except that I'm so overcome with good emotions that my body can't contain all of them. Bill smiles at me, reaches into his suit pocket and hands me a tissue. I keep on crying, and he keeps on handing me tissues.

Where is he getting all of these from, I wonder.

The image of my groom performing magic tricks at a magician show pops into my head. I have to stifle a giggle. I look at the pastor, and that helps me regain my composure. He is very old and very small. I am standing on a little hill in the grass. I'm tall anyway, and now up here, the pastor and Bill both have to look up to me.

"We need to get used to it," Bill quips.

That's my Bill, always wise-cracking. Always making me feel okay with whatever emotion is rushing through me at the moment. This time it is love; it is gratitude; it is hope. It is some precious feeling that combines all three of these and more. It is a feeling I have no word to describe. But I don't need one because I can tell that Bill feels it too.

Bill and I were one of the first couples to get married at the Leelanau Cultural Center. I remember we paid $300 for that privilege. Now it's a popular place for expensive, elaborate weddings with giant wedding parties organized by wedding planners, and people fly their guests in from all over the country. Back then, Bill and I were too busy to even go on a honeymoon. He was working and I was working and going to school. But our ceremony felt, and still feels, priceless to me.

Bill healed me. He helped me believe in myself, he helped me be a better parent and he brought me to my faith. I couldn't wait to become his wife. Marrying him was one of the best decisions I've ever made.

．．

The wedding was a week ago now. It was everything I ever dreamed of and more, and every time I re-live it, I get a swooning feeling deep in my chest.

Our life together feels like a new beginning for both of us. I know Bill has hurts and pain that he wants to put behind himself, just like I do. That is what is so precious about our relationship. We share the best parts of ourselves with each other, but we share the broken parts too. I've never been able to do that before. Not with anyone.

Yesterday I had to make the four-hour drive to Kalamazoo to deliver cherry juice concentrate to a new account—a health food store. Lately I've felt so torn. The kids need me but so does the business. So, I decided to take the kids with me, thinking I could multi-task and combine my work time with some much-needed family time. The plan was for me to make my delivery, and then Sam, Randy and I would do something fun together. When we arrived at the health food store, I was in such a hurry, and feeling so distracted, I accidentally shut Sam's hand in the door while unloading the concentrate. It was awful; the idea of causing my son pain because of my inattention made me feel sick to my stomach. I set the juice down on the sidewalk and comforted Sam. He wasn't hurt badly, and I think he recovered quicker that I did. But then I had to morph back into business-woman mode and make my delivery. Multi-tasking is not all it's cracked up to be. Or at least, not for me it isn't. This has become a lesson I will need to learn over and over again.

On the way home, I pulled off the highway so the three of us could stop for lunch. Just off the exit there was a Denny's, and I pulled into the parking lot, and the three of us piled out. The restaurant was busy, and we had to wait a long time just to talk to the hostess, and even longer to be seated. As I sat there with my boys, I realized just how small each of us really is in the whole scheme of things. There was the chatter of people around us, the clinking of glasses, and the constant hum of motion. I suddenly felt very small, almost as if I had vertigo. It was not a good feeling, and as I felt my anxiety build, I told the boys we were going to have to leave.

They both looked at me in a panic, and I was present enough to notice the disappointment in their small faces.

"But I really want those pancakes!" Randy blurted.

"Yeah, me too," Sam said.

I burst out laughing, and my anxiety vanished. Of course, we stayed. Of course, we ordered the pancakes. And, of course they were delicious.

Before Bill, before I stopped being so self-destructive and started working on my life, I know I wouldn't have been emotionally capable of appreciating this small moment of grace. Now I can. And that feels like a personal victory.

....

It is September 2001, that lovely moment with my boys is a distant memory, and my parents have just left to spend the winter in Florida at their condo. They are not just vacationing; they are heading south to hit the pavement and sell our cherry juice concentrate to new customers. My dad's theory is that most of our target market spends their winters in Florida, so why not go there and start opening store accounts? Plus, our bottle doesn't require refrigeration, so we know it will be a more compelling sale to the stores than other, competing products that do need refrigeration.

I so remember this time in my life. Back then the beverage market was very small, and most retailers did not have much refrigerator space that wasn't already full of milk, juice, and soda. It was only our first year in business and we'd made $64,000 in sales. The company was growing, not as fast as we wanted it to but, in hindsight, faster than we could afford. We did not know that our margins were way too thin. We did not know a lot of things back then. We only knew we had a great idea, a great team, and a great future.

I put myself back there, back in that time of excitement and worry. Since the business was started on credit cards, we are already behind the gun financially. Neither me nor my dad had other sources of income. The business was already struggling, and we knew it. However, that did not affect me much at first, as I was so sure of our future success. How could we not be successful? We were helping more and more people every day. We did the farm markets in the summer, the snowbirds ordered from our website in the winter, and when my parents got our product into stores in Florida, it would open up whole new markets for us. What, I asked myself, could possibly go wrong?!

This is my line of thinking, even though I am still in northern Michigan, it's gray and cold here, and I am struggling both emotionally and financially, and I fear I am losing faith.

Bill, the boys and I are supposed to leave Michigan's cold and damp fall weather behind too, and join my parents in Destin, Florida, for ten days, but I can't get my worry under control. I haven't received any checks at the business recently, and so I don't know how I'm going to pay the bills before we leave. If I ignore them and they sit here unpaid for ten days, I'm not sure what will happen. Will our phone get shut off? Will our suppliers stop doing business with us? I don't have my dad here to discuss this problem with, and I feel like everything just got dropped in my lap.

I pray and pray and pray for a solution, and when it doesn't come I think maybe I'm not praying hard enough. I know I have to take steps to help myself; I just don't know what those moves are. I have lots of good ideas, but there is one big problem with that: Every idea I have costs money.

My dad is always so positive. But sometimes I worry that his outgoing nature and all his socializing masks some real problems at the business. I've tried to talk to him about this, but he just says I worry too much. Maybe he's right, but I can't stop myself from doing it. Looking at our bank balance and our stack of unpaid bills sure doesn't help.

I know I need to learn how to detach. I know I need to stop worrying so much about things I have no control over. I just don't know how to do that. I've never known how to do that.

January 2002 dawns cold and clear, and after our trip to Florida I am back in northern Michigan feeling surprisingly optimistic. Bill helped me get a line of credit at the local community bank, and we've just been approved for a mortgage on the little harbor building where my office is, as well as on its sister building next door.

In the weeks to come, I open a little cherry retail store in the sister building. I develop a cherry skin care line and decorate the tiny store—only 200 square feet—to be cute and welcoming to both tourists and locals. It generates quite a bit of revenue for its small size—$250 to $500 dollars a day in the summer. It also provided us a nice cozy place to hold events. I'm also thrilled we have our own credit-card machine, so I can process orders as fast as they come in. We also have our own labels now, a reliable supply of juice concentrate to sell, and our cash flow is better. Not perfect, but something the Leland Cherry Company and I can live with for now.

By the end of 2002, the business had done $271,000 in sales. That sounds great, doesn't it? I thought so, too. Except that our loss was $53,000. This was mostly due to only having a twenty-percent gross margin and to the need to spend a great deal on marketing. The sales were rolling, yet we were sinking. We were not able to achieve a steady, predictable cash flow, I always owed more in bills than I had available in the checkbook, and yet since sales were moving along, I was making deposits and to me, in my inexperience, that felt like "cash flow."

By mid-January, I'm in a near panic, though. I call my dad, who is still in Florida, and share all of this with him. He tells me to relax, that this is just part of starting a new business. He acts like he was certain this is how it would go all along! I love his confidence. I just wish I had some of it.

With the line of credit, it does feel like some of the financial pressure has been lifted. Nothing is solved, but I feel

like things aren't as bad as they were before. I am an optimistic person and so I use that to calm myself. Things will get better. I am happier and less stressed at home, and that makes Bill and the boys happier, too. I try to be at work when I'm at work, and I try to leave it behind at the end of the day so that when I am home, I really am at home. I try to give Bill all of my attention when we talk, and do things with the boys instead of staring off into space and thinking about work. I'm not perfect at this, but I am getting better at it.

All problems, it turns out, have solutions. I need to learn to ask for help and not take everything on myself. For all of my life, that has been hard for me. I'm not sure why, but it has. I think it's because I'm an only child. My parents never treated me like a kid; they always treated me like a small adult, even when I was little. Which meant I was included in adult conversations and social situations with their friends, but also that I was privy to adult worries. That has stayed with me, and now as an actual adult, my instinct is to feel responsible for every problem, large and small.

When I was a little girl, I used to fantasize all the time about how great life would be when I was finally a grown up. Maybe this was because I spent so much time around adults instead of people my own age. Or, maybe it was because my parents never talked down to me, and expected a lot from me, even when I was a kid. Either way, I was convinced adults lived carefree lives filled with freedom and fun. Then, when I was planning the Leland Cherry Company, I used to fantasize about how quickly the business would achieve success. Oh, I knew I was going to have to work for it, but I thought my idea was so good, that my success was assured.

With both of these fantasies—the little girl who dreamed of freedom and the adult woman who dreamed of success—I was dead wrong. Not wrong to dream, but wrong about how automatic and easy freedom and success would be to achieve. Sure, adults have all kinds of freedom. Freedom to fail! And sure, I had a good idea. A really good idea. I just never considered that some people might not be ready for it. I didn't understand how great the need was for the market to be educated about the benefits of cherries, and I never thought others might actually try to steal my idea away.

....

It is now late summer 2002. A few months ago, a regional big box retailer had called and invited us to present our product to their buyer. We were nervous about it, but we were not sure why. This was what we'd always wanted, right? To have our product for sale in a big chain that covered a large territory and operated hundreds of stores. Because they are a successful Michigan-based grocery store chain with hundreds of stores, I was nervous about the meeting, but I was also beyond excited. Getting our concentrate stocked with this retailer could have made our company a huge success. My dad gave a presentation about our concentrate, showed off the product, and the buyer seemed interested. He told my dad he would call him in the next couple of days. We followed up with a thank-you note and phone calls, but for weeks we were told they hadn't made a decision yet and to check back later.

Well, I might have been confused about their lack of action back then, but now I know why.

It wasn't because they hadn't made a decision. It was because the buyer at the big box chain took our concentrate idea, took the bottle design we were using, and gave the chain's purchase order for cherry concentrate to the buyer's friend who'd decided to develop a competing product. To make matters worse, the buyer's friend found someone else to do the bottling, all while stealing our bottle design. That way, the chain could sell the juice cheaper and keep more of the profits for itself. They stole our idea and our packaging! When I learned the news, I spent the whole day feeling like someone punched me in the gut.

> **LESSON LEARNED**
> You can't protect an idea; you can only protect the physical manifestation of an idea. And even then, only if you pay an attorney to help you through the complicated patent process and your patent is granted.

There is so much more to know about the business world than I first thought. A good idea and a desire to make something that will help people is only the beginning. Never in my wildest dreams did I think a nightmare like this would happen. I was so naïve! Our bottle might not be our exclusive design—making that happen would cost thousands that we can't afford right now—but it is still our unique look. Why didn't I work harder to protect it? On September 3, 2002, I take out my frustrations in a business letter I send to the big box store. It allows me to express my anger but gets me no financial compensation. I finally received a letter back, which basically said, "Sorry, but don't try to fight us in court because our legal team is bigger than yours."

Here's where I am as 2002 draws to a close, a year that began with me feeling so optimistic. I owe a ton of money—the exact amount seems so large I avoid adding it up. I know we've lost $53,000 and our debts are at least $75,000 or more. Our margins are too small to get ahead, and the growth speed I was so proud of just months ago has us struggling to keep up.

We are out of bottles, and our attorney says there's nothing we can do about the chain's theft of our product and our design. I know I should feel sad, worried, and scared, but instead I'm beginning to get an inkling of what true entrepreneurial faith feels like. We are in a financial crunch, and I have been under-financed from the start. However, I had a great idea and made a business out of it that has made a lot of sales. I do know that sales do not equal profits, and I have to take draws to pay my bills, but I still think we can make it. My mom, my dad, Smitty, and I, along with Bill who is so full of support he is like a team member, will make it. My determination lives. I will find the money to help the business, I will live through this financial crunch, and both the business and I will be stronger because of it.

....

Time has passed. It is winter. Somehow, both the business and I have survived everything life has thrown at us. My marriage to Bill is stronger than ever. I am a loving and capable mom to Sam and Randy and they are thriving. But, while the Leland Cherry Company has also received my love and care, it has careened out of control. We are growing way too fast with no profit and to compensate, we are trying too many different sales channels and products for the amount of cash flow we have. I feel like we need to slow down and charge more, but we don't have time to do either. This is a brand-new product. If we charge too much, I am convinced that no one will buy it. As for me, I am stronger, I've learned a lot about running a business, which means I know enough to realize I need help. I need advice, but mostly I need money.

A solution—or what we think at the time is a solution—arrives seemingly out of thin air. Our phone rings and it is a representative from an infomercial production company. "Our producer wants to speak to you. He thinks your company could make a killing with an infomercial and he is so impressed with your product that he's willing to cut his rate down to almost nothing. You're so lucky! Most companies would do anything for an opportunity like this."

I'd never thought of selling our cherry concentrate on an infomercial, but it makes perfect sense. Older people use our product and older people watch more television than younger people. An infomercial would give someone time to explain the health benefits of cherries and make ordering easy for people who don't want to go to the store. The representative is right: It is the perfect venue for us!

For just $7,000 and dozens of cases of our product, the company, called BSN Enterprises, will script, film, produce, and air an infomercial for us. All we have to do is wait for the orders to roll in and fill them.

Bill, my dad, and I are so excited and we fly down to Pompano, Florida, where the production company's offices are. I'm going to be the spokesperson, and I can hardly wait for filming day to arrive. It does, and I spend a lot of time picking out my outfit, but no time at all on my hair or makeup. Surely, they'll have someone to do that for me, right? They don't, but I'm not too worried. We're filming in a beautiful seaside home and the director and his staff seem to know what they are doing. The shoot goes off without a hitch, Bill and I fly back to Michigan in anticipation of watching our infomercial on TV and having the orders roll in effortlessly, along with the profits.

A week goes by and we hear nothing. Then another week.

I call BSN Enterprises and they say our infomercial is almost finished and they'll be sending us a packet of information about stations and airdates very soon. Two more weeks go by, though, and we hear nothing. After dozens of my calls to them go unanswered, I finally get through. They've already aired our infomercial, they say. They cannot explain why we didn't get any orders; there were no guarantees. They stopped taking our calls after that.

It was a scam and I am both furious and devastated. We're out nearly $20,000—$7,000 in fees, the cost of our trip to Florida, plus more than $10,000 in product. Doing the infomercial at all was risky for us; now we're not going to make a dime from it. I tried to consider it a learning experience, but then three months later I got a phone call from another of BSN's victims. "Do you know your product is being sold on eBay?" he asked me. I checked and he was right. An eBay seller from New York was selling our product for pennies. And it was expired. I called the seller and begged him to take down his listing.

"It's expired!" I said. "It's no good anymore. It could make people sick." He said he didn't care. That he'd bought it at a fire sale and he was going to keep it on eBay until it sold.

I lost sleep with worry. Finally, I didn't know what else to do, so I called the FBI. An agent took down my information, but I didn't hear anything more. I thought it was the end of it, so Bill and I tried to move on. Then one day I was sitting with my dad on the little patio outside our offices, when a black Ford Taurus pulled up out front. Two men in black suits wearing black sunglasses got out of the car and walked toward us. In unison they pulled out their wallets and flipped them open to show their FBI badges. They asked me to tell them about the infomercial, so I did.

"These companies do this all the time," one of the agents said. "They comb the internet for startups. They take your money and move it offshore. Right now, it's probably on somebody's yacht."

LESSON LEARNED
When your parents told you that if something sounds too good to be true, it probably is, they were right.

I am in my car, driving up a winding and snow-covered road, and my fear is so large it is not just a feeling anymore, it is a being. I am trying to push Fear out the door and into the cold, but it does not want to go. Fear refuses to get out of my car and instead keeps its place in the passenger seat. I can't see him, but I can feel and hear him.

"You can't do it, turn around," Fear says.

I think of my husband and it gives me strength. Bill knows where I am going, he knows why, and he knows what I'm going to ask for. I try to replace Fear's command with his loving advice.

"Michelle," Bill told me, as I was walking out the door, "fear is only 'Future Events Appearing Real.'"

That sounded good, until I was in the car and on my way to do something I'd never done before: Ask an extremely really rich person for money.

The snow banks are too high for me to turn around, which is probably a good thing. And yet, if I did turn around without trying this last thing, the business would surely fold and I would be letting everyone down. Plus, how would I ever pay back all the money I owe?

I pull in a residential driveway and park. I stare out the icy windshield and take a deep breath, then force myself to get out of the car.

"Get back in," Fear says. "Just who do you think you are?"

The voice stops me in my snowy tracks, but the front door of the house opens and an older man named George—who I've always called "Mr. George"—invites me in. He is the grandfather of some friends from high school with whom I've stayed in touch. I first presented my business plan to his children; they told him about it and gave him the plan on a Saturday night. He called me last night and told me he'd read my plan and wanted to hear more. I was to be at his house at 9 a.m. sharp—he has church at 10—so he knows why I've come.

Inside, there is no small talk. He leads me into his study and doesn't ask about my children, and I don't ask about his wife. I am anticipating disaster, but this tall, handsome businessman says he has read my business plan, and that what I am trying to build is of some interest to him. Mr. George owns a cherry orchard and can see the value of my idea to farmers. He owns several companies, each one diverse yet dear to his heart. He thought my tart cherry concentrate business was a good fit with his portfolio. He might be 87, but he has modern ideas about the health benefits of certain foods. Plus, he told me he drank my product every day! He'd bought it in Florida, before we'd ever met.

> **LESSON LEARNED**
>
> **If you are not strong with numbers then find someone who is. Hone your strength and fill in your weaknesses.**

I can hardly believe what I am hearing. This is a last-ditch effort for me, one I had no assurance would work. I look out the window to steady myself. The view of Lake Michigan in winter gives me a surreal feeling, and the falling snow is mesmerizing. Next, he's going to want numbers, I'm sure of it, and my numbers aren't good. The fear returns, but instead of giving into it I pull my mind back to the present. He asks me about sales, about expenses, about our debt and about our loans. I've given him this information already—it's all in the business plan he's already read. Except the business plan looks into the future, and I am here to talk about the present. He tells me if he invests he needs to know what I am going to do with the money. I surprised myself by knowing the answers to all of his questions without even looking at my notes. I rattle off the numbers to him.

"Why are you here?" he asks me.

"I need $30,000 to pay our supplier or they are going to cut us off," I say. "No supply and we're out of business."

"I need to tell you something, Michelle," he says. "Once you take outside help, your business won't be your own anymore. So, think long and hard before you take a penny from anyone."

I say to Mr. George that I have thought about it, and I have come to a place where I either take the money or I go out of business. Mr. George looks at me for a long moment, then reaches down into his wastepaper basket and pulls out a crumpled piece of paper. He writes something on it and hands it to me. It's an IOU. He will be making me a loan of $30,000 that,

> **LESSON LEARNED**
> Be able to recognize good advice when you hear it. This was the most critical piece of information in my career to date, and I ignored it.

if I pay it back, will not dilute my ownership of the company. I tell him I will pay it back, a statement I believe with all my heart, even though I have nothing to back up that belief.

In fact, I did pay it back, then shortly after asked for another $30,000 and paid that back, too. I went to Mr. George one more time, but I could not pay off this third loan, and that was when he started taking equity in the company. What seems obvious to me now, but that I didn't know there in his den, was that each time we sold stock in our company, the amount of stock my dad and I had was diluted.

"Sign here," Mr. George tells me after we agreed on the first $30,000. "You'll receive a check in two days. When you do, send me a letter stating that your supplier is paid and send me some of your product."

I sign, and Mr. George stands up, looking at me expectantly. We'd concluded our business and our time was up. I need to leave so he could get to church on time. I stand on wobbly legs and hand him back the crumpled piece of paper. He escorts me to his front door, we say a polite goodbye, and I try to keep from weeping as I walk back out into the snow.

Maybe the tart cherry skin care line I've developed will be the thing to make us profitable, I think as I walk. Maybe with this infusion of cash I will be able to keep it stocked, keep all of our products stocked, and even develop new ones. I don't know it yet, but Mr. George will be a supporter of ours for a long, long time. I will grow to admire and respect him. He will pass his investment on to his son, who will not have any of his father's wisdom or commitment. But I don't know that now. I just know it is just beginning to get light out. The snow is still falling silently. The only sound is the door closing softly behind me.

It was December 21, 2003, and I'd just been given one of the best gifts of my life.

Money, yes, but it was more than that.

I'd been given a reprieve.

Bearing Fruit
2004 - 2008

*I*AM SITTING IN A RUSTIC CABIN TWEN-TY-THREE MILES NORTH OF MARQUETTE, Michigan, while Sam whittles with his new knife, Bill naps, and Randy relaxes on his bunk. After our debacle with BSN, we needed to get away from everything and connect again with what really mattered. Our up-north cabin for the week has a small porch, two small bedrooms, a basic kitchen and bathroom, but the cabin is so tiny that the bathroom's sink and mirror are part of the kitchen!

Ah, luxury. We have no television, no radio, and no clock. I'm still adjusting to that, yet it's also the part I like best about this vacation. It amazes me how time-driven we all are. Me especially. My hope is that, after some good days spent without the ability to mark the relentless passage of the hours, I will return home and return to work, refreshed and re-energized.

Since we arrived, I have been making a concerted effort not to think about work. Instead, I've done a great deal of thinking about taking better care of myself and taking better care of my family. I have so much desire inside of me to be successful, and I know in order to make that happen, I need to be a better, smarter, businesswoman. Today is the beginning of a new way of life. I have been spending way too much time focused on negative thoughts. So as of today, I am going to take better care of myself. I deserve to be successful, healthy, and loved. When I'm back home, I'm going to do more yoga, I'm going to walk more, and I'm going to take more time for myself.

I love my company and the potential it has, but I'm going to burn out if I don't live the rest of my life, too. And by that, I mean my life as a wife to Bill, as a mom to Sam and Randy, and as a person in my own right.

Tomorrow morning, we will get up early and go fishing. And I pledge to not think about work at all. From his bunk, Randy is looking at me funny. He catches me when my thoughts are a million miles away. This, I guess, is how good I am at not think-ing about work.

LESSON LEARNED

Learn to relax and shut off the stress of work—no matter how difficult this seems.

We did go fishing. A lot. And, we laughed a lot on that trip, too. But I wasn't able to keep work at bay. Several months prior to that week in the Upper Peninsula, my parents had gone out to dinner with another married couple they'd been friends with for years. Of course, the subject of the amazing health benefits of cherries came up in their conversation. My mom had an idea. "We think cherries would also be great for dogs," she said. That same night, after having dinner with my parents, my mother's friend went straight home and made a batch of dog biscuits. Except that this time, she added tart cherries. If cherries had health benefits for people, she and my mom had reasoned, why not for dogs, too?

The woman's husband had just sold his company, and the couple had cash on hand. She thought using some of that cash to start a dog biscuit business was a great idea. And me and my parents thought that if those dog biscuits had cherries in them, it would be a great idea for us to buy the exclusive rights to their product. She made some batches, then they went to a contract manufacturer.

As with other things, the idea might have been sound, but the execution wasn't well planned. That woman made dog biscuits by the truckload and even contracted with a manufacturer to make more.

> **LESSON LEARNED**
> **NEVER, NEVER buy more product than you need or can afford, especially if you are only doing it to appease someone else. And never, never go into business with others blind; get everything in writing.**

Since we had the rights, we felt obligated to buy them all. We did. And we were the ones who took the hit when they didn't sell. We were not capitalized for that kind of financial burden. Soon, we had no choice but to cut our losses. The couple ended up selling their company to a larger pet food company in Texas.

Looking back, I can see the mistakes we made and why we made them. In order to have exclusivity, we had to play their game . . . which meant buying whatever they manufactured. Or so we thought. There was definitely a market for the biscuits. This was when household pets were really starting to get attention at food trade shows. In retrospect, our timing was great! We just didn't have the marketing and advertising dollars to sell the amount of product we felt obligated to buy, fast enough. We also never discussed this problem with my parents' friends, asking them to slow down on supply. Plus, I'm not sure we needed to have exclusivity. We were already behind financially, and this deal made it worse. The product was a good one, however, and is still on the market today. And even though our partnership did not work out, dog treats were a more exciting sale to retailers than tart cherry concentrate, and pet people got the concept right away. It opened up new relationships with distributors and retailers that we maintained even after we no longer sold the dog biscuits.

What we also didn't know was that the U.S. Department of Agriculture regulates all consumer health claims—for products made for human consumption and products made for pets, too. We thought we were only stating factual information on tart cherries on the label, but if you put those facts on a product, the government says you are making a claim. And to make a claim you have to have the clinical trials to back it up. None of us knew this until it was too late, and because we'd begun a partnership with my parents' friends, I ended up spending a good part of our vacation week at that rustic cabin in the Upper Peninsula driving back and forth to a payphone so that I could talk to an agent at the Michigan Department of Agriculture.

Standing there in that phone booth brought back some painful memories. When I was a kid, my dad spent a lot of time on the phone for work during our family vacations. I'd hated that, and now here I was, doing the exact same thing to my own family.

I so needed to re-connect with Bill and the boys and re-charge my emotional battery. I had a lot of important meetings and some grueling business travel coming up in the next several months. I'd be away from Bill and the kids, so reconnecting now, like this, for a summer vacation in the wilderness of Michigan's Upper Peninsula was the best idea I'd had in a long, long time. I needed it. We needed it. And yet, I spent way too much time thinking about, planning for, and talking about, work.

After the week in the cabin was over, this is what I was thinking about on our way home: That the money from Mr. George, my first investor, saved our company. That was just fact, plain and simple. But that was three whole years ago. The Leland Cherry Company now needed one more infusion of cash, and as soon as I could get back home, I'd need to figure out where it would come from. Great sales and great profits were coming very soon; I just knew it. All we needed was one more chunk of money.

The dog biscuit decision was another example of us being in over our heads, operationally and financially. By the end of 2005, we'd had $697,000 in sales with a net loss of $223,000. Our receivables were $59,000 but our payables were $132,000. We were growing the "top line," as they say . . . our revenue . . . but our expenses were growing as well.

I kept asking myself, Could I go back to Mr. George? I hadn't decided that yet. Looking back with a clear eye, I know now that this was when I should have reached out for advice on what it means to take investor money in order to keep your business going. I did not know at the time that doing so, and then trying to break away, would be worse than a divorce. You need money to build and grow a business. Everyone knows that. But you also need money to break away from your investors. That's the part no one thinks about until it is too late.

Either way, I had doubts but I willed myself to believe we would prevail. We had to. Leland Cherry Company was ready to become a big success. Weren't we?

. . . .

I cannot believe how fast time flies. I'm back at work now and that week in the U.P. feels like a distant memory now; like travel to some remote and rustic planet. I've been traveling for work, but it's all been to big cities, not to cabins in the woods. This fall I've been to Baltimore, then New York, then California, to exhibit at trade shows. The biggest show of the year for products like ours is the Natural Products Show in California and its sister show in Baltimore. I also went to a practitioner show in New York. From then on, we did at least six shows a year. We'd set up a booth, and I'd demonstrate our product to the staff from retailers and distributors who were attending the show and just looking for the latest and greatest to stock or sell. It was a good plan, but not so successful for us since we did not have funds to support any of the programs needed to play in that arena. For example, United Natural Foods is the biggest natural food distributor in the country, they distributed us, and they require you to participate in their trade shows and promotions. The show in California alone cost us $15,000.

Sometimes these were smart expenditures—like when we were able to sell to Whole Foods and other large chains—but sometimes they were not, and it was impossible to tell until you did the show. At one time, our cherry concentrate was sold in more than 2,000 stores. We also had a private label company that was in Canada.

LESSON LEARNED

Being married to an entrepreneur is like being married to a rock star — the spouse ends up coming in second.

I traveled so much during that time. I missed Bill and the boys, and I know they missed me, too, but I just kept telling myself that I was doing the right thing. That Bill and the boys miss me, and I them, but all this traveling is for them. I wanted to make a success of the company not just for me, but for them, too.

Besides the stress of travel, I had something else to deal with, too. Something big. We'd received a letter from the FDA warning us about making health claims regarding tart cherries. About this time there were at least thirty other companies that had also started selling tart cherry products for uses other than desserts and pie filling. The ones I asked said that they'd received the letters, too. None of us knew that we were breaking the law—we were just putting research information on our labels. Later I found out that one company had been selling a cherry product with "prevents cancer" on the label. An FDA inspector saw the label and reported it, which launched an investigation into all companies that sold cherry-related health products. We had to spend thousands on new labels and new marketing materials.

In the meantime, I was still traveling and so was my dad. All that travel meant making frequent use of our company credit cards. You'd think after several years in business I'd be familiar with all the rules and regulations regarding these business tools. After all, I'd funded our start-up with them! Well, not so. Here's something related to credit cards that I actually did not know: If you are an American Express business account holder, it is not okay to pay yourself through your merchant account.

You know those swipe machines stores use to sell you things? All that means is that they have a merchant account with the credit card company, and not just a consumer account. If you have a merchant account with American Express, and if you are an officer of the company that has the account, you are not allowed to swipe your own merchant machine. This rule can be found in the sixteen-page merchant agreement. Printed so small you'd need a microscope to read it.

Desperate measures come from blind determination. I was just trying to fund the company any way we could. Visa, MasterCard, and Discover will all let you do this, no problem, but do not ever, ever try it with American Express. If you do, they will shut down every American Express credit card attached to your name and your company, including the one that your dad has in his wallet and is trying to use to pay for the gas he just pumped into his company car. This is the company car he has driven on his regular sales route, to make his regular deliveries, and to take his regular orders. But this time his card is declined by the gas station's cash register.

"Michelle," my dad asked me over the phone, "what's going on with the Amex? I just got declined."

He was on the road, selling, and at first my dad just sounded curious and mildly annoyed, but then he became agitated, and I didn't blame him. He worked as hard as I did, and now he was stuck miles from home with a car full of gas he couldn't pay for unless he used his personal credit card. It was embarrassing.

On my end it was a big, "Uh oh, what have we done?" moment. This was no small thing, either. We ended up having to go without American Express for a few years. It was times like these when I felt glad for my strong faith. Despite everything, I believe I had grown more spiritually in the past year than I had in my whole life. Believing God is omnipotent helped me live in the present and solve problems—like my dad being stranded at the pump.

....

We had other problems to deal with, too. Our first investor, Mr. George, was getting older and by 2008, he said he wanted us to find other funding. When he bought into our company, something else came, too: board meetings. When you have an equity investor you also get a board of directors. And when you have a board of directors, you have to have board of director meetings. I was terrible at this. I had no idea what a board meeting entailed, and because our accounting books were always so disorganized, I'd need to spend hours with a hired accountant beforehand trying to figure out what the numbers meant. The accountant did his best, but I could only afford to hire him for a few hours at a time, so the next month I'd have to repeat the process all over again. I would be frantically trying to understand why we had such a big loss; it seemed like we were always writing off inventory, a bookkeeping strategy I did not understand.

Then I'd print out our statements at the last possible moment, often as the board members were walking into the conference room. By the time the meeting started, I was already frazzled.

As Mr. George aged, I was sent out to raise money. I had the energy and the desire, but I had no idea how the process worked. I went out on the funding circuit by myself with zero experience and very little preparation. I was petrified. And yet, after traveling from coast to coast to raise money, I was successful. It would take years, but I would finally acquire my first "angel investor" in 2008.

Looking back now, I think this was the beginning of the end for our company. And I had no idea. I was in so far over my head that I felt like someone told me, "Here you go, there are 250 passengers on that plane, now go fly it." There were times when I would be landing in New York City, scheduled to make yet another presentation to venture capitalists, and I felt so anxious that as the plane glided over the Hudson River, I would think to myself, "Maybe we will crash. At least then I won't have to give my presentation."

There was so much riding on my securing money that I was scared out of my wits. I felt so much responsibility to others, and I felt like I had no support at all from the board of directors.

In the meantime, we were looking for buyers—wholesale and retail—for our concentrate. In 2002, my dad went for the first time to Expo West, one of the biggest natural products retail trade shows in the country. My dad flew to California, and that first year we didn't exhibit, he just walked the aisles and checked out the products and the way they were being marketed and met as many people as he could. One of the people he met was a guy named Dave. He had been in the nutritional sales business for about five years, had already built up a customer base, and he and my dad hit it off right away. Dave had a large account in Germany, and the people who ran the company were actually looking for a source of cherry concentrate. My dad called to tell me this, and I could hardly believe it. It was the first time at this show and bam, a huge order. We were over the moon.

There was, however, only one problem. The German company wanted the concentrate bottled in a very specific aluminum bottle. (We won a packaging award for that bottle in Packaging Digest.) We found a supplier for the bottle, but we could not find anyone with the proper equipment to cap the bottle once it was filled with our concentrate. That was a challenge, but my dad and I remained undaunted. This was a big order that could lead to more big orders, and we were determined to fill it.

We found a company outside Chicago that would build us a capping machine. It was too expensive for us to buy outright, so we made a deal with the bottling company that if they built the machine, we would pay them back per bottle. Meaning, they would get a few cents for every bottle they capped until we'd paid off the cost of building this very specialized machine. My dad called Dave, Dave called his contact in Germany, and the deal was struck.

We waited and waited and waited. No machine. We called and asked. No machine. We called and complained. No machine. Finally, I called and told the capping machine manufacturing company that this order was time sensitive, and that I was driving, that very day, from Leland, Michigan, to their offices to pick up my machine and they'd better have it ready. They said okay, and I hit the road. Half way to Illinois, I got a call. Not only was the machine not ready, it wasn't even in the United States. A company in Taiwan was building it, and it hadn't even been loaded onto the boat yet. I was crushed. I pulled into a gas station and called my dad.

"We're sunk," I told him. "We're never going to be able to fill this order without that machine." My dad agreed, but then he had an idea. Perhaps there was a prototype of the machine somewhere in the U.S. that we could borrow instead. I called the cap manufacturing company back and asked. Not only was there a prototype, it was in the Midwest and I could have it. I got back in my car and headed for Richmond, Indiana. Once there I strode into a warehouse, introduced myself, and tried to describe an esoteric capping machine prototype. At first, the people at the warehouse had no idea who I was or what I was talking about, but eventually they found it at the back of the warehouse in an unmarked crate.

It was huge. How was I supposed to fit it into my car? I wasn't. The warehouse loaded it onto a truck and I would follow behind, all the way to our bottling company in Henning, Illinois. We were going to be able to fill a $250,000 order. I called Dave out in California with the news. His German customer will be able to launch their new product because I made it happen.

"Don't worry," Dave tells me, sounding furious. "They've canceled."

I was stunned. We had so much riding on that order. It could make or break us. And, it had just broken us, or so I felt at the time.

I pulled over to the side of the highway. Cars whizzed by one after the other inches from my door. This was the moment I thought about stepping into traffic. When I'd left home, I was $30,000 in debt. Now I was almost $300,000 in the red. I spent several minutes feeling sorry for myself, and then I called Bill.

"Congratulations!" he said. "Yesterday, you were stressed that you were $30,000 in debt and now you are $300,000. How many people can do that in one day?" He was so supportive of how hard I'd worked that it snapped me out of paralysis and into reality. I called Dave back. He called his customer. We offered to ship the product for free and they accepted. We lost money on the deal, but we filled the order as promised.

. . . .

Despite this very real financial scare, there is a new strategy I'm trying out. Some people might call it dreaming—as in the now comfortingly familiar, "Michelle, get your head out of the clouds!"—but I call it visioning. And in my new vision for my life and for the company, this happens:

I get the biggest check we've ever received. It is a $50,000 down payment on a $102,000 invoice. The business is on a total and permanent upswing. We are finally profitable, and everyone is going to get a raise for Christmas. We have received our first dividend check. It is awesome. I love what I do, I love the money I am able to make, I love helping people and all the good I am able to do with our company.

Bill and I have a new house, designed the way we have always wanted it to be with a big 2,300-square-foot house with a large kitchen and dining room all in one big area. We have a nice master bedroom with an attached writing, yoga, and art room. The boys have a great big bedroom they share, but that can be divided up easily if they want a bit of privacy. We have a big loft with an office for Bill and me to do anything we choose. We have a great den with a bedroom and one other room for Bill's kids to stay in when they come to visit, which they do frequently. The yard is beautifully landscaped with a big herb garden and a peaceful sitting area. Our home is filled with love.

LESSON LEARNED

When you feel like you are panicking, do something productive. Take action even if that action is only in your mind.

I try something called "Productive Dreaming." Here's how it works: Instead of obsessing over a problem, or in my case, multiple problems, you focus on the way you'd like things to be and on solutions for achieving that reality. In my mind, the Leland Cherry Company gets more new orders every day. We have a newsletter going out this week to hundreds of thousands of customers. We are profitable and our debt is slowly decreasing. We are thriving in our industry, writing dividend checks, and paying our many employees big bonuses. We have attracted good deals, strong margins, and everyone involved in the Leland Cherry Company is happy to be along for this rewarding ride.

The theory behind productive dreaming is that you can't achieve what you want if you don't know what that is. And I am convinced. Someday, this won't be a dream, it will be my—our—reality.

Which tells me one thing: I need to dream bigger. I've been reading two books, one from the past and one that's new. The Science of Getting Rich, by Wallace D. Wattles, which was published in 1909, and The Secret, by Rhonda Byrne, which was published this year, 2006. My thought is that if I can learn from these books, I will not have my current struggles and will make enough money to keep my business going and do good in the world. The ideas inside these books were published almost a century apart, and yet they share a common theme. Decide what you want, commit to it, fill your efforts with passion, and receive the results with gratitude. I can do this. I've even made my very own gratitude jar! It is just a big glass jar I emptied and washed and decorated with yarn, but it has become a visual reminder of everything I am grateful for in my life. So, I have decided what I want, I've committed to it, my efforts are filled with passion, and I'm so grateful for every little thing I've received. The only thing that has been stopping me from getting the whole of what I want is faith. I have that now, so here goes:

When I am 45 years old, I will be a millionaire. I will have money for Sam and Randy's college and for Bill and me to travel the world. We will have a foundation that helps people set up their own businesses and helps educate them on best practices after they do. I will be a writer and an artist and I will get my inspiration from all the traveling I do with Bill. The Leland

Cherry Company will be wildly successful, both financially and ethically, and our company will be known worldwide for helping people who suffer from arthritis, gout, exercise fatigue, and even some currently unknown ailments. Sam and Randy will love college, and both of them will find their life's passion. My parents will be financially set, and so any worry they once had about money will disappear. With their financial challenges over, any other problems they currently struggle with will be solved. I will be mentally strong and emotionally peaceful. And my faith in God will be unshaken.

Do I know how to dream big, or what?

....

Sometime after my focused dreaming, the company's credit cards begin to get declined. We are all out of bottles, out of juice concentrate, and out of the pill form of concentrate we'd just developed and that were actually selling well. Our suppliers will not re-stock us until we pay our past-due balances, which I would have done, willingly, if I had the money. We were quite excited about the big sale we'd just made to a new customer, Dan, and it seemed like this large order was just a preview of the things to come. Then his $65,000 cashiers check that he'd sent by overnight courier bounced. So, he's got plenty of our products at wholesale prices that he can re-sell for a nice profit, and we've got nothing but bank fees and unpaid bills.

As soon as I learn about his bad check, I spend the morning researching him. Unbeknownst to us, he'd taken advantage of a number of other small companies just like ours. Basically, he's a crook. Something I would have known if I hadn't been so blinded by the prospect of a big sale that I didn't even think to check him out. Instead, I sent him product on credit because I believed him when he told me, over the phone, that he was good for it.

Despite all of our money worries, we need to keep working. Life, business, the retail world does not stop just because our credit card got declined or a big check from a new customer bounced. So, we've signed up to present at Expo West again. This show has been a good one for us in the past, and I know it could be an awesome business

opportunity for us this year, too. It is the best way we've found to get our name and our products out to new markets in an efficient way. But with a $65,000 bad debt, how am I supposed to pay for our travel? Our company is growing quickly. Maybe too quickly. By 2008, we had sales of more than $950,000.

I need to be more skeptical of people I don't know, instead of being so naive and trusting. I thought the buyer at that big box store taught me that lesson when he stole my idea and my design, but I guess I needed to learn it a second time. With that situation, I complained but I did not fight it. Here's what's different: With Dan, I'm going to fight him with everything I have. That man is going to pay his invoice in full. If he doesn't, I'm going to sic my dad and Bill on him. My heroes.

When I look back on all the anxiety this incident produced for me and for everyone at the company, I remember how protective my dad is of me and a feeling of calm comes over me. I did end up having to turn this bad debt over to my dad to pursue. And although no one believed he'd be able to get our money back, he did get it back. Every penny, including our attorney fees.

My dad and I made a good team back then. He is better at schmoozing than I am, better at conflict resolution, but he can also be tough when tough is called for.

After that, I remember closing my office door, sitting down at my desk, and closing my eyes. Thanks to my dad, I knew we were going to ExpoWest, and that's all there was to it.

....

There's someone else who cares just as much for me. There's someone else who protects me and watches over me. Someone Bill introduced me to, and someone I need to talk to about my problems a lot more often—God!

> *Dear God,*
>
> *Today I would like to hand over all my worries and fears to you.*
>
> *I am sure that only good can come my way and that you will provide.*
>
> *I pray that we have a good, prosperous show. I pray we can attract the right investors for us. I pray to help pay back all the people who have helped me make my dreams come true.*
>
> *I believe that our company has a great deal of value and we will do just fine.*
>
> *I am a money magnet.*
>
> *Everything I touch turns to gold and I am abundant and full of love. Amen.*

....

Months pass. Things go well, and things go awry. I work long hours and I take days off. The Leland Cherry Company makes sales, and sometimes we pay our bills on time and sometimes we aren't able to. Bill and I settle into our lives, mostly happy with each other but sometimes not, and the boys grow.

As they do, I commit to teaching them lessons from my own life experience. Like, for instance, the value of a dollar. Don't be like mom and spend too much when you're flush with cash. Save money so you'll have it when you need it later. That's the lesson I'd like them to learn, and that Bill has tried to teach me. I'd like them to grow up to be responsible adults who plan for the future, instead of just living on enthusiasm and thinking only about today.

Did my parents try to teach me that? If they did, the lesson didn't take.

One year about this time on New Year's Eve, Bill and I went to dinner at the Leland Lodge with Sam, Randy, Bill's sister, Joyce Marlene, and his brother-in-law, Leo. The Leland Lodge is a charming, sprawling restaurant on a golf course and is known for its delicious Midwestern fare. The six of us are in a festive mood; I'm ready to say goodbye to a difficult year and think good thoughts about the future. Bill is happy to be with his family, and the boys are feeling special for being allowed out at night at a nice restaurant with the adults.

The hostess seats us at a big round table, gives us cloth napkins, and hands out great big menus. I watch the boys open their menus very seriously and then start to read through their choices. Lake trout, smoked ribs, roast chicken, and steak.

Near the bottom of the list of entrées is the most expensive choice. Lamb chops for $35.

"Those look good," Sam says, licking his lips.

I have never served lamb chops at home, so I don't know if he is testing

LESSON LEARNED
You can grow yourself right out of business. Sounds counterintuitive, but it is true. Don't take sales for granted. Seek good financial counsel.

me by choosing the most expensive item, or if he would really like to try this new dish. It's a special night, a holiday, we are all together, and things at the company are doing, if not well, at least we are holding our own.

"Go for it," I tell him.

Sam is quiet for a moment, his head down, the corner of his lower lip wedged between his teeth, a pose I recognize as his when he is in deep thinking mode.

He looks up and breaks his silence.

"Hey," he tells the whole table. "How about you give me the $35?"

"Yeah," Randy adds, "And we'll go home and make ourselves some sandwiches."

The whole table laughs, but no one smiles bigger than me. I guess my lessons are getting through. Eventually, both will go to college and graduate with accounting degrees.

Growing Season
2009 - 2012

WHO WOULD HAVE THOUGHT THAT ME, A GIRL ALWAYS SO TRANSFIXED by nature, always looking for faces and shapes in the clouds, always drawing and painting her feelings, would someday become obsessed with cold, hard numbers? Not me, but then again, everyone says life is full of surprises. The storyteller in me thinks that's why we all want to keep on living as long as we can. To experience the twists and turns and then find out how the story ends.

Maybe saying that I've become obsessed with numbers isn't exactly accurate.

Actually, I'm obsessed with numbers when there is a dollar sign in front of those numbers. It's not that I've become materialistic; it's that I now have a better understanding of what money can do for a new company.

In 2009, the Leland Cherry Company entered its eighth year of business, and we reincorporated as "Michelle's Miracle Inc." In our first eight years, I have raised and lost a total of $1.2 million. Does that amount of money faze me? No, it does not. As a matter of fact, I am about to try to raise another million-plus, if things go according to plan. Which is this: Even though the United States is suffering the worst economic times since the 1920s, and even though I am looking for people to invest in

the healing properties of a tiny fruit, our current investors—
Mr. George's son and Lauren from my angel investor, PAF—
have decided to send me out alone again, with no training and
no financial backing, to raise more money. It's a hard thing for
me to admit, but Lauren and Mr. George's son are now calling
the shots. Making the decisions. I now own less than half of
the company I founded. The minute you take money from an
investor, that is what happens. And they are expecting more
and more from me, even though they put in less and less. I'm
comfortable selling my product to customers—that is actually
my favorite part of my job—but now I have to "sell" my business idea and myself to people who have money to risk on us. I
don't know how to talk numbers, I am trying my best to learn as
fast as I can, but I am afraid of sounding desperate. Desperation
does not inspire confidence, and confidence is a key ingredient
to attracting outside investment.

I do know that the money itself isn't the end goal; how it's
going to be used for my company is. We'd like to expand into
more stores and hire more salespeople. We'd like to develop new
products, make our brand a household name, and help as many
people as we can. If I am successful, I will be replacing myself
because we will have the money to hire a more experienced
CEO, and I would transition into being the company spokesperson. I'd be highlighted as the founder, but someone else would
be handling the business. I have mixed feelings about this, but it
would probably be for the best.

But, as good as those plans for growth and expansion definitely sound, I know now there is a darker side to all of that
investment money. And at night, when I am alone with my
thoughts and praying for guidance, that darker side can sometimes seem overwhelming to me. I was starting to figure out
that each time I accepted investment money, I sold a piece of my
soul. And yet, what alternative did I have?

I lie in bed next to Bill, who has fallen into a restful sleep, and think about my options. I feel like my role in my own company is being bulldozed underground. I have a couple of choices for new funding, but I'm not sure I have thought them through. I'm not sure that taking all this investment money in exchange for shares of the company, and then not sticking up for myself with the investors, is the best thing for me or for anyone involved.

God, I am asking you for guidance. Please help me be strong enough to follow my dreams. Please help me to be smarter! Help me to stay optimistic and motivated. Help me not to give up.

• •

I must have finally fallen asleep, because it is morning. Even though Bill is still next to me, I feel like he is miles away. Or, maybe he's the one who is here and it is me who is miles away. Man, these last few months have been so stressful. In 2009 the company received a big investment—$150,000! I had presented our story to an angel fund. I'd done many other presentations that had not gone well. One of these had been in a high rise in New York, and I was so overcome by an anxiety attack, I'd wanted to jump out the window of the conference room. And we were on the twenty-second floor! But this presentation to a venture capital firm out of Wisconsin that invests in women and minority-owned or -managed businesses in the Midwest had gone much better.

Our contact at the fund was the fund's co-founder and managing director, Lauren. I have a lot of respect for Lauren because she successfully built a tech company, sold it, and is now re-investing in companies like ours. But I'm also more than a little intimidated by her. I can take constructive criticism, but she is demanding that I be the one to raise more money, and this seems nonsensical to me. It pulls me away from what I am best at … sales and educating customers about the amazing benefits of tart cherries. When the angel fund initially offered us funding, neither my dad nor I liked the fund's terms, so we turned their offer down. Then when it looked like their offer was the only angel capital we were going to get, we went back to them to reapply.

"If we do make you another offer, it will be the last time we do," Lauren promised. "And, the terms have changed."

By that Lauren meant the terms of their offer of money had changed. Not to benefit us, not to benefit Michelle's Miracle, but to benefit the investment fund. Their first offer had been more money for us and less ownership for them. Their second offer was less money for us, and they took more control of the company. Even though they would now have much more decision-making power, our choice was not a good one. We could either accept their offer or not get funded. And if we didn't get funded, there was a very real chance back then that we would have gone out of business. Looking back, had I known that Mr. George's son would make that threat nearly every six months for the next seven years, I might have risked turning their offer down.

In retrospect, I should have paid more attention to the change in terms, but I was too preoccupied with making my company a success to look too hard at the deal. It should have been a red flag to me that I was about to sign my company over to a bully. I'd already lost a majority share when Mr. George took an equity stake after we became unable to pay back his loan. Now I was losing even more control. But we needed the money to stay alive and to grow, Mr. George's son advised me to just sign the damn thing because this angel fund was the only one offering any new capital. In the weeks prior, I had gone to New York and Madison to make similar pitches for funding, and I thought these had all gone really well. Those feelings had been confirmed when the head of the fund called to follow up. "Michelle, it was great to hear your pitch, and we would like to see you again." I was so excited! There I was in New York City, making deals with the big shots, and I thought, "Look at me, I can do this after all." Fifteen minutes later, the same women called back. "I'm sorry, Michelle, I was supposed to call a different company." Then she hung up.

I felt devastated, and that moment would stay with me for years afterward. It was with this mindset that I accepted the offer from Lauren and her angel fund.

....

That was just one of the experiences with financing that made me into what I call a "hindsight expert." During this time there was a great deal of wasted money that went not to building Michelle's Miracle, but rather to pad the pockets of all the legal and accounting "experts" that the angel fund required we use. These people cost the company thousands of dollars that could have been saved by hiring less expensive firms. Even before she was officially on board, Lauren wanted me to make drastic decisions about the direction of the company, often while we were right in the middle of a negotiation. It felt dangerous to me even then to be counting on one person to keep my dream alive, and as it turned out, my intuition was spot on. I never did get the management expertise the angel fund promised me, but I did get the criticism when things went wrong.

....

Maybe leveling harsh criticism is how every angel funder operates, but I was too inexperienced to know if that were true. It is easy, even today, for me to feel as if I am right back there.

Lauren's management style is not confidence-building; it is confidence-destroying. She makes me so nervous that I make mistakes and stop seeing things clearly. My head hurts. I feel like I could pass out. My heart is just banging. I know I am projecting bad energy even though I really don't want to.

At home, Bill tries his best to calm me. He says to hang in there, that there will be a payoff, but for the first time I am not so sure about that anymore. Intellectually I've known for a while that I've given up my decision-making power, but emotionally I feel like I've given up control over all aspects of my life. I'm learning that everything in life is a trade-off. On the one hand, my company is so close to making it big! But on the other hand, my team, including myself, is perilously close to breaking. Lauren has been very candid with me about the management and financial holes in the company, and I know she's right in many ways, but how smart is it to close a first round of funding with only $100,000 when we need at least $200,000? She says we'll get the rest in six months, but we need it now, not six months from now! And yet, I'm still being told about all the changes we need to make.

LESSON LEARNED

Listen to your gut, it is always right.

We finally close the financing with Lauren's fund on the last day of March 2009. Yes, this month came in like a worried little lamb, but we are going out like a lion! I have decided, once again, to do my best to put all my negative thoughts aside and focus on the positive. I am concerned that we need more capital, but with this new round of funding from the angel fund, I am hopeful that we will get to do what we've been dreaming about for the past eight years: Tell the world about the power of cherries. And that feels so exciting!

Back then, I had no idea that I would have such little say

in how this new capital would be spent. I wanted to launch a new and much-needed marketing campaign to retailers and consumers. Instead, it was the investors who had the power to decide what to spend the money on. I trusted their expertise, but looking back, I see now that it went to everything but marketing. It went to pay the legal and financial experts and make payments on loans provided by the investors they had forced us to hire. Most of these were the funders' friends and colleagues.

....

My dad is having surgery today. The same day we close on the new financing. He's been struggling with pain in his knee for too long. Sitting here in the airport waiting for my flight to the East Coast, I'm excited for the company to be funded, and I'm excited for my dad to be pain-free. After his recovery, we are hopeful that he will finally be able to walk comfortably again.

I'm on my way to New Jersey to give a presentation at one of our distributors' tabletop shows. A tabletop trade show is where all the vendors of a particular distributor are invited to set up a booth to showcase their products to visiting retailers. I'm excited about attending. It is the first time I can remember leaving town on a business trip and not being worried about the unpaid bills I'm leaving behind. As soon as we close on the funding, we will pay all our vendors and brokers. It is difficult to describe the relief I feel over being able to do that. I like the feeling of owning my own business, of building a company from scratch, of being able to raise capital in such a rough economic time—something I bet very few people can do right now—but I hate owing people money. And not being able to pay them back. My honesty and open communication helps me retain these retailers and buyers.

I arrive in New Jersey in full anticipation mode. This is what I love to do—educate people about the healing properties of tart cherry juice concentrate. Unfortunately, that's not how I spent most of my time at the show. Instead, I was on the phone with the fund's attorney and our attorney so we could finally close the deal.

Why did I think I was up for this? Why?

The uncertainty was stressful. As soon as I landed, I had a couple of drinks, and then I drank two glasses of wine on an empty stomach. What had me so worried was that the information about the new financing that I needed was back at my office. I had failed to bring it with me. This was something our investors should have been helping me with, but they weren't. I never did eat dinner, and the night before the show I started feeling really sick. On the day of the show, I was supposed to be staffing our booth and representing the company, meeting new people, and getting new customers, and instead I spent the entire day throwing up and racing to the bathroom. Basically, I missed the whole show. My nerves had taken a toll.

We eventually do officially close on the new funding, and the money is finally in our account. And yet I also know it is going to go right back out again. That was two days ago now, and I still feel sick to my stomach. . . . I have to apologize to the people who worked for our broker. Their booth was right next to mine, and they watched my booth for me while I took phone calls from attorneys and ran back and forth to the bathroom.

Now that I'm back home, I know I have to make some tough decisions. I have to control my habit of self-medicating—drinking—during stressful times, and I have to cut expenses at work. I'm not sure how I am going to do this, because we are already a pretty lean operation. The new funding is being spent in large sums on attorneys and a part-timer who is supposedly our new CEO, but as far as I can tell, it isn't accomplishing anything. I am doing my job to market the company and to be a spokesperson, but I am also still doing the tasks required of a company president. And yet I am not really calling the shots at all. I am a puppet, patted on the head and sent out to do the same things over and over again, with different results expected. Isn't this the definition of insanity?!

I am actually thinking of quitting my job. I'm thinking of leaving the company I founded. I've been worried and anxious before, but never this bad. I've told myself over and over again that the way I am dealing with stress is not good for me, and that I have to quit before it takes me out. That's my personal goal. At work, my goal is to drastically cut our costs. Lauren told me to do this even before she came on board. She has constantly repeated this message since.

· ·

Yesterday I fired Becky. I had to do it, the company couldn't afford to keep her on, we don't have money for any extra staff, what we really need is a qualified trained bookkeeper, and she doesn't have those skills. Logically all those things are true, but that didn't make doing it any easier. Becky has been with the company since 2004 and she handled our bookkeeping. Our staffing is already too small, and now I don't have her to depend on. The only other people here are my mom, who handles customer service, my dad, who's in charge of sales and marketing and helps me communicate with the board, and one of my closest friends, a woman named Judy who is a part-timer in charge of shipping. Eventually Judy would prove to be a valuable asset to the company and become full-time. Over the years, Becky and I have become friends, and now I had to fire her. I know it is for the good of the company, but I feel terrible about it. She feels terrible, too, and that's probably why right after I fired her, we got drunk together. At the office.

My personal net worth was about $28,000; our investors have millions. I didn't understand how the world worked. I didn't understand how investment worked. I was naïve to think we stood a chance of being equal with them.

In addition to my sweat-equity, my parents were eventually able to put a great deal of money into the company, but we still could not keep up. We even took cash advances on credit cards, out of necessity, just to keep up with the investors. Bill had put in a large chunk of his money, too. In hindsight I know that there was no way for us to keep up with all our expenses and obligations, and keep our stock, so we went into personal debt as well. As a family, we did everything we could.

LESSON LEARNED

Intense feelings of stress and anxiety are part of the process of starting and growing a business. Find healthy ways to deal with them.

I am supposed to be preparing for a monthly board meeting—this has long been a task of mine, but now that the angel fund is on board the intensity of my responsibilities has been ramped up—but there is absolutely no way I can be productive today. I have a lump in the dark pit of my heart, my mouth is dry as dirt, and the office smells like a missing friend. Or else, stale cigarettes and spilled beer. Take your pick. I am sad about having to sacrifice Becky's job, but I don't have time to think about her absence because I am under too much pressure to perform.

Cut expenses Michelle. Where are the sales Michelle? Go raise money Michelle. Fire your friend Michelle.

I did not think this was what owning your own business would be like.

Before working with Mr. George's son and Lauren and her angel fund, I had no idea what a board of directors was, what they did, or how their meetings worked. Now, I know more than I ever imagined about all those things. For example, here's what a board meeting is like when you've sold your soul for a large investment: At this point, I had single investment deposits that were as high as $250,000 and have raised close to $4 million. I have a $900,000 line of credit. The board consists of me, two members from Mr. George's Family Fund, and two members from Lauren's PAF. In order to facilitate communication, I once tried to bring two of our sales brokers with me to a board meeting. The board belittled me so severely the brokers came to my defense. They'd come along to update the board on our sales success, and instead they were defending my character. The board, in my mind, had become like uncaged predators, out to get me.

Geography didn't help. My board members were from all over the country, I was supposed to choose a central location for the meetings, and, for those who couldn't make it in person, make sure that the central location had a conference room equipped with a conference-calling phone. Next, I had to notify the board members when and where the meeting would be and call all of them to ask if they had any agenda items to add to the schedule. Then I had to prepare the agenda. In order to do that I needed to compile all of the company's most recent financial statements, down to the penny, in order to show the directors what I'd spent their money on. Since, by this time, I had put my life savings and my new husband's life savings into the company—about $150,000—it was my money, too. I didn't object to this being part of my responsibility. What I objected to was having no help to do it. I didn't have a secretary, a personal assistant, or an office manager. I had me. And I was expected to do all of this, with no slowdown in my other responsibilities.

Here's what I knew: I was more motivated to make Michelle's Miracle successful than anybody, but the directors didn't want to discuss that at our meetings. They wanted results, not planning or idea generation, and they wanted those results yesterday. They did not want to strategize. They wanted their money back, and they wanted it back without giving one thought to what needed to be done at the company to make it profitable. The same people putting their money in needed to be engaged. They were not.

Here's what I found myself thinking: I wish I knew how to do all this. I wish I knew how to read a financial statement, how to keep track of financial documents and accounting programs. I know I've been in this now for almost a decade, but I've been so busy working I haven't had time to learn any of this and there is no one to teach me. Numbers have always been a nightmare for me, and I have never had business accounting training. I could understand the profit-and-loss statement, but the balance sheet was a mystery to me. I couldn't understand why it was so important that I know how to do everything, when part of what the investors were supposed to bring to the deal was financial and management expertise. I'd given up control of my company, but I was still expected to create product, make sales, raise money, prepare for board meetings, go to shows, and do store demonstrations. I wish I were better at math, and better at running meetings, and better able to communicate my ideas. Because that's how the Leland Cherry Company—now Michelle's Miracle, Inc.—started out, with one of my good ideas. I was the one observant enough to notice how people were clamoring for the cherry processing plant's by-product. I was the one who cared enough to ask these people to tell me about how they were using it. I wasn't sure at first that I even wanted my own business—I would have been happy with a raise! But the plant I was working for wasn't interested in my idea. Only when I was sure of that did I branch out on my own. No one ever showed me how to make a go of it; I've learned how on my own by jumping in first and asking questions later. My strength has always been my passion to help people; not to be a businesswoman.

That working style functioned okay at first, and yes, it has gotten us this far, but it's not going to work anymore. I know that. What I don't know is how to grow into my new role, and even whether I am capable of it. There is so much to learn, but I can't take time away from all my other responsibilities in order to learn it. I tried to communicate that to the board members today, at my board meeting, but they were not interested in hearing much of what I had to say.

I'd done all the organizing for the meeting in advance, found us a conference room in Grand Rapids, made sure their meeting packet and their lunch were waiting for them when they arrived, and yes, set up the room and made sure there was hot tea and coffee available, too.

Note to self, and to anyone else with a good idea—no, a great idea—that's looking for funding: Venture capitalists do not care if this is the first time you have run a board meeting. They care if your receivables are growing, and they don't care if the company is growing too fast. They do not care if you just wrote a $10,000 order on the way to the board meeting. If you tell them about it, they will not express pride, or enthusiasm, or give you an atta-girl. Instead, they will ask you when you will be writing a $10 million order. And then they will tell you what kind of sandwich to order for their lunch.

Another note to self, and to anyone else who gets venture capital for their great idea, but not enough venture capital to grow their business, so they must go to the bank for a loan to augment their venture capital: The banker you discuss your loan application with will not be the same banker who helps you fill out the application, and that person will not be the same banker who calls you to approve your loan, and then the banker who

LESSON LEARNED

Before you agree to venture capital, know what a board of directors is supposed to do and what they can control.

calls you to say you are in default on the loan will again not be the same banker. And when you ask why they are categorizing your loan as being in default, because you have made every payment and plan to continue doing so, the banker will tell you that the balance statements you submitted to the bank four bankers ago are simply not robust enough today. And, of course, even if you do get a bank loan, it will take weeks to be approved. And if you are like me, your company needs the money now.

Bill and the boys have been incredibly supportive *of* me, and so patient *with* me. For the past year my focus has been on securing money for the company so that we can pay our debts, pay our operating costs, but also so we can spend some real money on marketing, product development, and business travel to get the word out to retailers. No matter how good a new product is, no one is going to benefit from it if they don't even know it exists. In just a few months, I've been to California, Chicago, Grand Rapids, New Jersey, New York, and Washington D.C., to attend trade shows and do product demonstrations in an effort to raise more funds. Some of these trips have gone well and the meetings and shows were worth the time and expense. Others have gone less well, and I won't be doing them again. But regardless of where I'm headed and why, I know I can count on Bill to make sure everything runs smoothly at home. I know that Sam and Randy will be fed, that they will have help with their homework, they'll make it to school, and to their practices, and to any special events, on time and well loved.

But I miss them so very much! They are the true miracles in my life, and I am not with them. I want to make them proud and create a successful company, but I think I am fooling myself at this point.

I'm thinking about this while sitting in my economy-class seat waiting for my flight to San Francisco to be airborne. Bill is the only reason I'm even on this flight. Lauren and the board agreed I'd go to this conference hosted by Investor's Circle, a group established to fund entrepreneurs with ideas that support a sustainable economy. Since Michelle's Miracle, Inc., provides cherry farmers with a new source of revenue, we might fit the bill, and I was excited about presenting. But when I tried to book my flight, my credit card was declined. This is the kind of thing Becky used to handle, but without Becky to keep bills paid, I was losing track of days. I turned to Bill, and he booked my flight with his personal credit card.

I am now headed two-thousand miles cross-country to ask a group of sophisticated venture capitalists for money, with nothing in my wallet but a twenty-dollar bill. I must be getting used to this seat-of-your-pants financial existence, because I don't even feel too bad about it. In order to save money, I'm sharing a room with another applicant. She is all excited about the financing process, about her pitch, but I am not excited at all. With this trip, it has all started to seem so fake to me.

And yet I know we are so close to breaking this business wide open. We've raised $1.3 million. That figure seems so large until I think about how undercapitalized we are. I'm going to have to talk to Lauren when I get home and explain that we can only cut our expenses so much. Last week, our Internet got shut off because of a $99 overdue bill. I am running a million-dollar company, and I don't even have a credit card that can pay for our Internet so we can process orders and pay for my flight to San Francisco so that I can go ask for more money. If anyone would have told me, eight years ago, that this would be a snapshot of my finances today, I would never, ever have believed them.

If I don't get another round of funding from this Investor's

Circle, Lauren is going to have to pony up. We are about to explode with new business. I can feel it.

· ·

The spring and early summer of 2009 passed. Lauren never did invest more money in us. What she did manage to do was drive a wedge between my dad and me that lasted for too long. She also brought in other, smaller investors, which might have seemed like a good idea to her, but it only made our financials and our management more complicated. Two banks turned our loan applications down, but we started emailing offers to our retail accounts every week, and that always brought in sales. The economic climate was particularly tough; some of our customers were behind on their bills, and the emails encouraged them to pay so that they could re-order. The emails also brought in new business.

One day, we got a $68,000 order from a large private-label account we'd had as a regular customer since 2005, and then we got a few other big orders, too, and those came at just the right time. In essence, they saved us. At least temporarily. My presentations to the staff at venture capital funds got better and better but didn't lead to any more investment. I was doing my best, but we really needed a good financial person to "close" the pitch, and we didn't have anyone like that on staff, nor were any of the board members willing to come and help.

By the end of June, pressure from work began to manifest itself in physical symptoms. I'd stopped doing yoga, and I'd stopped exercising. I felt like there wasn't time, and I certainly didn't have the energy. Once I'd been a marathon runner; now I was exhausted all the time and thirty pounds overweight. The migraine headaches that used to show up once or twice a year would attack two or three times a month. I started suffering from insomnia, and I had no energy for Bill or the boys. Not even on weekends, when I was supposed to be turning toward them and away from work.

Instead, my Blackberry was never far from my sight. In fact, I'd become addicted to it. One weekend we invited a broker from Chicago to visit us and stay for a meeting. While sitting at a casual dinner outside by the fire, I was talking about how much my Blackberry was controlling me. "I need to get rid of it," I said. The broker nodded. "Do you really want to get rid of it?" he asked. "Yes!" I said. And just like that, he took it out of my hand and threw it into the fire! It burned up, and, instead of anger, I felt instantly relieved.

Just when it seemed like things really couldn't get much worse, my first investor, Mr. George, died. It was June 28, 2009. When I heard the news, a wave of sadness and regret passed over me. He was so wise, and the first person outside of my family to believe in my idea. He was also the one who'd said, "Michelle, once you take outside help, your business won't be your own anymore. So, think long and hard before you take a penny from anyone." His children had taken over managing the investment in our company, but I missed him. He lived out of town but would always come see me several times whenever he was in Leland. No one else ever did that, not even once.

I'd listened back then to what he'd said about outside money, but the full weight of his words all those years ago on that snowy, desperate morning were completely lost on me then. I was too inexperienced in business to understand what he really meant.

If I had known how right he was, would I have done anything differently?

I can honestly say I don't know.

What I do know is that I will miss him. His family has said they still want to be involved with the company. I hope that's the case. Because he understood what I was trying to do with Michelle's Miracle, he was wise in the ways of the business world, and he tried to share some of that wisdom with me.

Not knowing how to do something is no excuse for not doing it. If 2009 taught me anything—anything at all—it was that.

Don't know how to make a presentation in front of 200 investors after driving eleven hours straight for the privilege of standing on a stage in a wrinkled suit? Do it anyway. Don't know how to launch a new product in new packaging that your competition hasn't even thought of? Do it anyway. Don't know how to wrap up a conference call with your board of directors so that you can make the ceremony inducting your sons into the National Honor Society on time? Do it anyway. Don't know how to apply for seed money from the State of Michigan and navigate its ridiculous and so counter-intuitive bureaucracy? Do it anyway.

And solely because I chose this life that often pushed me into anxiety-producing activities, whether I wanted to operate like that or not, this is how 2010 began: With the biggest single investment ever deposited into our company account. The State of Michigan has confidence in the power of cherries, grown here, to both help people heal and to help cherry farmers make a better living off their land. They proved that right before Christmas by staking us with a $250,000 investment. I was so excited… I took a photograph of the check. That's the good news.

For a business, the opposite of "good" isn't "bad," it is "stress."

And the stressful news is that there is now even more to get done, and there are now even more people who have invested in Michelle's Miracle, Inc., and will want to know what I've been able to produce with their money. Most stressful of all? I cannot do anything without the approval of the board of directors, and they are far too busy to engage with either me or the company. They are happy to critique my performance after the fact but are unavailable when I need advice.

I'm happy for the money. I'm happy we will be able to overtly re-brand the Leland Cherry Company over to our new name, "Michelle's Miracle." There's a good reason for this decision. When we started out as the Leland Cherry Company, my parents and I soon realized we'd need more of a distinctive brand. We had an old logo from a restaurant our family had owned called, "Michelle's Café," and used it. Then we realized that the name and the brand should really be the same. Eventually the brand name was changed to Cherry Works. I'd hated that name. What we had with Michelle's Miracle was a cute little brand that needed a good accountant and a marketing budget. It had a loyal following. I have so many letters from happy customers, and on days that I didn't think I could take the stress one more second, I would either get a call or a letter thanking me for supplying them with our tart cherry concentrate. When those calls or letters came in, they always gave me a shot of courage to go on for one more day.

I'm happy we can pay our suppliers and hire a vice president of finance to manage our increasingly complex accounting. However, he turned out to be useless and lasted less than a year. I'm happy my own salary will be paid regularly instead of just here and there when the company can afford it. I am not happy being president and CEO. I was supposed to be replaced by someone more experienced so I can do more of what I do best, educate the public on the benefits of tart cherries. I do that, better than anyone. The board's solution to this is assigning me to raise money to replace myself. They want to remove me as CEO and I don't care. I'd like to focus on being a full-time spokesperson. I know now it would have been a positive change—I'd shown I was quite good on TV, especially live TV.

Why wouldn't I be? I got to brag about my baby and how good she was! I was fast on my feet, too. Northern Michigan hosts an annual celebration, the National Cherry Festival, and I was often invited to be a guest on the news and talk about cherries or demonstrate recipes. One year I was doing a live morning news show segment where I was supposed to mix up a cherry smoothie. At the last minute, I realized the top to my blender was missing. I saw a paper plate on the ground, picked it up, covered it with my hand, whispered to the newsperson "don't drink this," and blended with a smile on my face.

I loved doing events and demonstrations. I loved meeting people. And when I did this, sales went up. I wanted to be the company spokesperson, but before I could do that full time, I had to raise money to pay the person who would replace me. I have since learned that, while frowned upon by business experts, it isn't all that uncommon. When you take money from outside people and organizations and don't really understand their intention, bad things happen. There is always a "but."

I had no idea what an emotional and physical toll that would take.

My back hurts, I'm still getting migraines, and I rarely sleep more than four or five hours at a stretch. I'm exhausted. It is going to take more than money to make Michelle's Miracle, Inc., the success I know it can be. It is also going to take a great influx of human energy. Where is that energy going to come from? Some days I couldn't even get out of bed and just sobbed.

....

Doom and gloom. This gray feeling seems so thick to me now that I cannot see the greatness in anything. I know we have so much to feel blessed for, but I don't feel the blessings, because I am far too focused on the gloom. Michelle's Miracle is busier than ever, or we would be if we could fill all the orders we've received. This is the first time in ten years that our supply has been so short. There was a crop failure in 2002 and again in 2012, a freak spring storm decimated the tart cherry crop we depend on.

Cash is short as usual, but we are carving the budget like crazy. I know I will not give up, so why do I feel so down all the time? I get lost within my own thoughts, within my fears, my regrets, and mostly within the guilt and remorse I feel for some of the choices I've made. I am in over my head with the investment piece, and it is killing me. Maybe this is just how a person sheds pain in order to get to the joy, but I don't see a way through. I pray for guidance, but this time, I am not sure that anyone is listening.

··

Even though my official title at the company is still the same, "President and CEO," I've thought of myself as company spokesperson since day one. It feels strange to have to try to raise the salary money to replace myself, but I hope I am successful. From the day our incorporation papers arrived in the mail on March 23, 2001, that's the real role I've played for the company. I'm the person who talks! The one who knows and cares the most about our products. Heck, practically every piece of clothing I own is red now. For a brief time, we did hire a CEO, Ann. She did nothing but give me to-do lists and create chaos and attorney bills. First Ann was on the board, where she was an asset. Then she was made CEO and was terrible at it. She lasted less than a year, and then they secretly brought on Richard, who later secretly brought on Meghan.

I talked to cherry processors, and farmers, and grocers, and people at senior centers. I talked to investment bankers and marathon runners, soccer moms and radio show hosts, Cherry Festival tourists and community leaders, agriculture professors and government officials. On and on. You name a group, and either I already have, or I would be willing to, talk about cherries with them. I believe in our product, so none of this was particularly difficult for me (except maybe my contacts with the investment bankers—they're so serious). Plus, talking numbers was not and never will be my strength. This is why we really need an engaged accountant who can talk numbers and who understands marketing. That was the most important thing we needed in our company.

A few months ago, I started taking cherry concentrate myself; I drank it every day and without fail, and I've gone from being an enthusiastic spokesperson to a fervent convert. Prior to that, I was too busy to think about taking care of myself. At Bill's insistence, I finally went to the doctor for my back pain and the migraines. My diagnosis was severe degenerative disc disease and attention deficit disorder, which I know were both exacerbated by stress. I was prescribed a lot of medication and was told I'd be on it for a long time and perhaps the rest of my life. Later, I was diagnosed with "Sympathetic Dominance," meaning I was in flight or fight mode all the time. For a full year, I was in so much pain Bill could not even hug me.

I tried the medication for a short time but did not like the idea of being on so many pills, and so I took myself off them all, cold turkey. I would not advise this . . . I went through incredibly bad withdrawals. The withdrawals were so bad, I spent my time in a hotel room with the worst flu symptoms of my life. It was the boys' 18th birthday. So much time lost. So instead, I decided to at least try our own remedy, and, it worked! Our cherry concentrate helped a great deal with my back pain, and it has lessened the severity and frequency of the migraines, too. I have never believed in our company more than I do right now. I am truly the best spokesperson for our company even though I am still expected to be "president." In my role as spokesperson, I am making products come off the shelf by creating a connection with the consumer. That was something I was really good at—no . . . I was great at it. Instead, I spent too much of my time stuck behind a desk crunching numbers I did not fully understand.

Looking back, there are some things about this time that I still do not understand. What I do understand is this: from 2008 to 2012, I was spread way too thin, I lost credibility, and our competition went sailing by us and captured market share.

When we started there was very little competition, most of the cherry farmers in northern Michigan and elsewhere didn't believe cherries could be sold as a product with a medicinal benefit, and most people did not even know about it. About a year after we started, many new companies that did want to capitalize on this benefit popped up. There was a crop failure in 2002 that wiped out most of them, but new ones eventually took their place. We had a great supplier, who was so great they ended up being one of our main competitors. While I was out chasing my tail raising money, the competition was gaining momentum.

> **LESSON LEARNED**
>
> **Be aware of your competition. If you think you don't have time, make time. It matters. Make time to research, follow and know.**

Any success we had in gaining new accounts was almost always just after I'd spent time being an active spokesperson, though those opportunities were not as numerous as I would have liked. When I was out talking up our products, the board meetings were more productive because I had good news to share: Our sales were climbing, and the re-branding was going well. All along, this should have been my official role with the company.

When I was a little girl, I was creative and had an active imagination. At some point not only did I lose that, but I lost what I am beginning to think was the real me. Free-spirited and free-willed to do good. I think that was taken from me by all my responsibilities, or else I just seemed to lose sight of it somehow. My new quest is to find my true self. Taking charge of management and company financials felt to me like being told to fly a 747 with 250 passengers on the plane with not one hour of flight school.

The board and some of our investors have tried to make me into someone I'm not. Even Ann, before she became our CEO and while she was still on the board, pressured me to be more analytical and less creative. I know she has a lot of experience and expertise, but how am I supposed to learn anything from her when she won't even let me finish a sentence? It is difficult to ask a question when you're constantly interrupted.

> **LESSON LEARNED**
> Should you be president of your company? What does leadership mean? Don't assume you should be president just because you are the founder. There may be better uses for your skills.

....

If I thought the board was hard to work with before, it has become even harder after Ann became CEO. She openly dismissed my ideas and me so often, she has a hand gesture to use instead of addressing me out loud. When I open my mouth to suggest something, she lifts a hand and flicks it in the air and says, "I got it, I got it!" It has become so obvious Bill and I frequently use it sarcastically on each other at home, and then break into bittersweet laughter. My creativity should have been valued for the growth of the company. That was how we started and managed to make $1.5 million in sales. The brand had personality and what's called a "sticky following." Meaning, people buy our product over and over again, despite price or competition.

The new board member and everyone else can try to make me a number-cruncher, but that is not who I am at heart. I'm a storyteller. I want to actively seek out consumer shows and other speaking opportunities and relinquish my title of president to someone else. I know the board of directors wants this, too, but they are too disengaged to be much help in making it happen. When the Leelanau Horticultural Society gave me their Distinguished Service Award, they said they chose me because of how well I represented the cherry industry in northern Michigan. So, it isn't just me who thinks this is my natural calling; it is other people who value orchards, too.

Having someone else become president of the company did sound extreme to me at first, but it would mean I'd be stepping back and relinquishing any control. What it would mean is that I would return to working more intently toward my original goal when I started the company: To help people by sharing the healing power of tart cherries.

Our original investors must be feeling some of the same enthusiasm that I am. That and God is looking out for us and for the farmers who sell to us. Because 2010 ended the way that 2009 did—with an investment in an amount we could have only dreamed of back when my dad and I founded the company. Thank you, God, for answering my prayers and for believing in me. On Dec. 12, 2010, we closed on $900,000 in investment capital in the form of a line of credit, for which the family of our original investor, Mr. George's son, co-signed and continued to fund. I have now raised almost $4 million on my good idea, my ability to talk about my good idea, and my ability to get other people to understand just how good cherry juice concentrate is for the human body.

Not bad for a girl everyone said was too scatterbrained to run a business, because she always had her head stuck in the clouds. They were right. I do spend a lot of my time daydreaming, even now. But you know what? I'm here to say that there's nothing like the view from up here.

I'll hold tight to my plan of someday passing my leadership responsibilities onto someone else, but I can't do that just yet. Michelle's Miracle still needs my leadership. No one else cares as much as I do or has had my experience. The board wants me out of this role, but they are too disengaged to make anything happen. And no matter how much the stress of building this company wears me down, I will not give up. There is no one else to do it. I cannot give up. No one else loves this company as much as I do, and no one else will work as hard as I will to make her a success.

I can tell the stress of all that money and all those investors who want a say in what we do with it is getting to me, because I've started drinking again. If I am honest with myself, I'll admit I never really stopped. Weeks, and sometimes even months would go by without me having a drink, but then our supply would run low, or my dad and I would get into a power struggle over something we should not be at odds over, or an order I was expecting wouldn't come in, or our sales numbers would be too low, and I'd reach for alcohol to dull the stress.

It's a common belief that drinkers have to hit rock bottom before they ever really stop drinking for good. I always believed that, too, and since I'd never been down that low, I didn't think I needed to quit. I also didn't think hitting rock bottom meant hitting a hard surface with your head! But, that's me, always taking everything so literally.

· ·

The day in late June started out like every other day. I woke up early, made breakfast and lunches for my boys, Bill and I spent some time in conversation, and then I headed to the office. Once I got to work, the accounts needed to be balanced, I had a dozen phone calls to return, and a couple of bad checks to deal with, and there was something wrong with the online order form. It wasn't working properly, and people coming to our website could not place their orders.

Ann had been appointed CEO and I was trying my best to learn how to work with her, but not making much progress. She offered me no advice, only criticism. She was being paid $50,000 a year and I could

not see what the company was getting in return beyond her habit of making lists of things for me to do. And she worked from her home in Illinois. What we needed was a good accountant. We had a part-timer who was doing as much as he could with limited hours. He had the skills we needed, and had been helping me devise marketing strategies, and I could not understand why the board didn't bring him on in a more official capacity. Instead, they actually let him go. We didn't have anybody doing numbers for a while. At a board meeting in Chicago, I could feel a distinct coldness in the room. At one point, Ann threw a stack of papers up in the air and said, "I can't even get decent numbers!" Right, I thought, because the people who could give them to her had all been let go! After the meeting was over, no one said anything to me. I cried all the way back to Michigan. I knew my days were coming to an end.

By the time I got home that day, I had zero energy to make dinner, so I opened a bottle of wine instead. And then I opened another one. And then I got drunk, and then I fell down, hard. I bumped my head, wrenched my neck, scraped my cheek, and hurt my hand. The next morning, I woke up and thought, God is not whispering to me anymore, he is yelling. I was taking on so much stress and responsibility for others that I ended up drinking the night away to dull the fear. Bill always said that God would tick at you, then tick a few more times, then level a few whacks, then wham! The thing that finally changes you will happen.

That fall on June 20 was my rock bottom. I was done with using alcohol as a crutch. And I meant it this time. It was the best thing I could do for myself, and for my family, and for my business.

I knew there would continue to be other people in my life who drank to excess, and I knew they would have to make the decision of whether to quit for themselves. As for me, I was done with it. To live healthy, to be a loving wife and mother, and to run a business, I needed a clear head. I could do this. I could run a company, and help it grow, without turning to alcohol, no matter how stressful things got.

· ·

Three months after I changed my habits, I came up against the first real test of my resolve. It's September, and here I was in Grand Rapids writing, reading, and preparing for a big meeting with Ann to plan the company's 2012 budget. Our work together feels barely okay and certainly not great. Working with Ann is extremely stressful. She doesn't listen. Well, I should qualify that. She doesn't listen to me. I have ideas, but she is more interested in talking at me than with me. I am worried, and this process is causing me anxiety, but I am experiencing those feelings as a healthy person. It sure feels good to know I can face challenges without drinking away my fear. Thank you, God. I love and appreciate my freedom from alcohol. When I stopped drinking, I had no idea how my life would change for the better. Yes, life can be difficult. Yes, Michelle's Miracle is still struggling to make a profit, and yet I feel safe and mostly at peace. I feel in control—if not in control of the company, then at least in control of myself.

God, I want a drink! Or something to take this stress and fear away. Today was awful. I started my first week of work in 2012 with this bit of news: the board of directors is auditing Michelle's Miracle. As if that were not bad enough, just before Christmas the board informed me that I would no longer be able to sign checks or any other official company document. I found out later that Ann and the board had a meeting with Richard without my knowledge. Richard came to the office to "audit" us a few days later. His assessment was that we needed better margins. That was our biggest problem. The board's solution? To make him CEO. Our new chief financial officer will be handling all of that from now on. It's my company, I started it, and it's got my name on it, but apparently those three facts are not enough of a reason for me to have any financial or legal input. And, since bad things come in three's, here's the worst of it: In two weeks, a report of the audit from the board will be served to the heirs of Mr. George, my first investor. They will then have to decide whether my company will continue to exist. Leading up to this decision, no one from the board and none of the supposed "experts" I had been forced to use asked me a single question. They made decisions without me and did not communicate those decisions with me.

LESSON LEARNED

Do not use a third party that is not close to the industry you are in. Especially for accounting!

I feel sick, and I'd love to cure that sick feeling with a drink. I am scared as hell about what is happening.

But I know no matter how good that first sip tastes, it would only be a temporary cure, and that knowledge is what keeps me from doing it. I want to, but I won't. I want to, but I won't. I say this refrain to myself over and over again until I believe it.

· ·

The company's destiny is in the hands of Mr. George's heirs, our original investors, since they are the only ones putting money in. Although I have been able to see some of the numbers, I have no decision-making power and even my ideas are sidelined. I've sold too much stock and lost too much control to matter any-more. Richard, our new CEO, has decided that he cannot deal with my non-business personality. In the beginning he would say, "Michelle I am going to make you a business person." My thought was, "Why? That is your job." Mine is to be creative with recipes, trade shows, sales, and marketing. I know I can't do or say anything to sway their business decision, one way, or the other. I have no power over the future of a company I started. I only own eleven percent now.

LESSON LEARNED
Businesses aren't living creatures. Too much emotion leads to poor decision making.

It's a strange feeling, but I'm not giving up. I refuse to believe this is the end.

For three days I wait. Three excruciating days. Will the company even be a company anymore? Or will it cease to exist? After all my work and sacrifice and stress and joy, Michelle's Miracle isn't a bank account and an office and a product to me, it is a living, breathing being. And I can't bear to imagine that it—she—might die.

· ·

Two weeks go by, and I have been far too busy working to

celebrate my company's reprieves with the people who have supported me the most. Not our investors, but Bill and my parents. But then on a cold, snowy evening in March, Bill and I go to my parents' house for dinner. We are all so relieved that the company has dodged all of these dangerous obstacles, at least for the time being, that we stay up way too late. By the time dinner is over, and I am cajoling Bill that it is time to go home, the snow has piled halfway up their front door.

We push it away, pull on our boots, trudge to our car, and make it out of my parents' long driveway and onto M-22, finally headed for home in the muffled dark. I look out the back windshield and see the snow is like a winter wake unfurling behind us, blowing and drifting up almost as high as the side windows of our car. I turn back around and look out the front windshield just in time to see that a huge tree has fallen right in the middle of the road.

"Bill!" I yell.

"What?" he yells back.

"Tree!" I reply.

"It's okay," he says, in his calm, normal voice, "I got it."

And then my stable, dependable, reasonable husband casually maneuvers our car around the tree at the last possible second in the middle of a snowstorm in the middle of the night.

"When did you see the tree?" I ask him after my voice returns and my heart rate approaches something like normal.

"Right after you said, 'Tree!'" he answers, and we both start laughing.

It is pretty funny, and we are still laughing fifteen minutes later when we drive in our driveway. There is a lesson here, too, that I'll never forget. It is okay to speak up. Even when something seems like it should be obvious, you might actually be the only one noticing danger or coming up with a new idea or thinking up a solution to a problem.

Now when I get a gut feeling, I try to speak up more. Sometimes it is helpful, and other times it causes conflict, but standing up for myself is still a goal of mine. I'm sensitive to criticism, and so it isn't easy for me to speak my mind when I disagree with someone, but I make a point of doing it anyway. It was Nelson Mandela who said that courage is not the absence of fear, but rather the triumph over it. I need to stop worrying so much about what I can't do and start doing what I can.

Bearing Fruit
2013 - 2015

I AM SITTING IN MCGUIRK ARENA ON THE CAMPUS OF CENTRAL MICHIGAN UNIVERSITY (CMU). An awards dinner for successful entrepreneurs is underway and, believe it or not, *I* am the awardee. Me, Michelle White, the woman with no math sense, no formal business training, and no interest in finance. And yet, CMU's Research Corporation (CMU-RC) has just named me their Entrepreneur of the Year.

"Our annual selection of Entrepreneur of the Year allows for recognition of key entrepreneurs for their sacrifice and commitment," I hear Erin O'Brien, the president of CMU-RC, say into a microphone while the audience listens politely. "2013 was a rough year for the tart cherry industry following a crop failure in 2012, and White's entrepreneurial drive not only allowed her company to maintain but to grow sales by 36 percent."

Erin then says that I exemplify the innovative spirit needed to accelerate economic development in regional agriculture. I hear those words and I see the expectant faces on the people in the audience, and I wish I could tell them how hard this has been. I wish I could tell them how many mistakes I've made, how easily the "money people" have taken advantage of me, and how hard this has been on my family.

But that is not the story they want to hear.

"It is an honor to be chosen for this award," I say instead, when it is my turn to speak. That is how I feel, it is an honor, but I feel other things, too. Those I keep to myself.

"I built this company with the vision to help others, and as a non-farming female, I have created a successful business in spite of what the industry believed could be achieved. I am very proud of that." I was also a woman, working in a traditionally male-minded, male-dominated industry that believed cherries were only for dessert and health food was a tiny market. At the beginning, no one wanted to hear what I had to say. But I kept going. That to me was success, even if we were in a desperate financial struggle.

Before the ceremony, I'd received a letter from CMU to announce the award. Of course, I was thrilled and proud and I showed the letter to everyone in the office. Yes, they were giving the award to me, but I also felt like everyone who'd worked at Michelle's Miracle had contributed. When I handed it to Richard, our new CEO, to read, he skimmed it quickly then handed it back saying, "Well, it's not really an award, is it?" At the ceremony Erin had handed me the award made of a glass ball etched with my name on it. I put the award in the center of my desk and kept it there. To me it was tangible proof that Richard was wrong. About the award not being an award, but about a lot of other things, too. At the end of 2013, our sales were up. We'd done $1,474,000 in sales over the past year, with a loss of $140,000. Despite everything, we were making progress. Our losses were decreasing.

....

Michelle's Miracle has a slogan—"discover the power of tart cherries"—and, by 2014, four signature products: Original Tart Cherry Concentrate, Joint Formula, Sleep Formula, and Tart CherriMax Dietary Supplement. All four (created by me and my dad) are 100 percent natural with no preservatives, no food coloring, no additives, and no added sugar. Scientists at Michigan State University, whose research was funded by the United States Department of Agriculture, have discovered a substance called "anthocyanins" in tart cherries. Anthocyanins are plant pigments loaded with antioxidants, melatonin, and potassium. The scientists published their research in professional journals, confirming what the people coming to the plant for our cast-off juice knew all those years ago: That two tablespoons of tart cherry juice concentrate are equivalent to an aspirin.

I feel vindicated when I hear about the science, but I didn't need it to know that cherries could help people feel better.

I also feel regret. In order to get the company to the place it is now, I've had to give up most of my ownership. I own only about eleven percent of my company—a figure I've said aloud to myself yet still find hard to accept. I'm just a minority shareholder and have very little say in how the company is run. Even though I am still the one who knows the most about our products and our customers!

The market for our products is vast—I truly believe that only a small fraction of people knows anything at all about the healing capabilities of cherries—and yet I feel constrained in my ability to reach even a fraction of that market. Farmers, wholesalers, and retailers are beginning to catch on, but the general public does not understand the importance of quality in this "new" product; not all tart cherry juice concentrate is made equal. And when I started this company, I was the only person who believed in this product. Now that we have created a market, we have competition. Their products are not as pure or of the same quality that ours are, but I'm worried that won't matter to an uneducated public. All the board cares about is securing more and more funding; I want to turn our attention to our customers.

The reason they want to secure funding is so that they can

get their investment back, with interest. I disagree. I want to use any funding we do receive to reinvest into the company. This disagreement has caused a rift between myself, the board, and our investors. Richard is on the side of the investors, I am on the side of helping our customers; my parents, who both still work for the company, are caught in the middle. Richard personifies my inner critic, and in his eyes, I can do no right. Just last week I asked him, "Who is our target audience?" and he could not answer me. These people do not care about helping others; they only care about themselves.

LESSON LEARNED

Do not share details of your business with strangers, even if you think they want to help you. You can get help without revealing trade secrets.

If I thought Ann or Richard was bad for the company, or impossible to work with, Frank was worse.

I met Frank at Expo West; he was at a booth next to us. My back tension was through the roof and I learned he was an acupuncturist, and he said he could help me. "Can you help me right here?" I asked. "Not today," he said, "but I will bring my bag with me tomorrow and we will get you fixed up." Awesome, I thought! I have finally met someone that gets me. Frank made good on his promise. The next day he came back to his booth with his bag and administered acupuncture on me. While he was doing his thing, I was chatting away about cherries. He was asking questions and I was confiding that we needed new formulas, and that I was taking a lot of heat from my board and had only so many resources. The pressure on me from Richard was so high at that time. Richard was constantly saying that Mr. George's son was going to shut the company down if sales didn't increase. I was desperate to find someone to help me. Frank was a doctor;

I thought I could trust him, and because of that, I told him more than I should have.

Frank was hired by the board as a formulator. He was supposed to help us develop new products, but he was a power-hungry person and soon capitalized on the doubt in my abilities that the board was already feeling. He saw Michelle's Miracle as an opportunity for him, and he wanted me out, so that he could take over. He and Richard began having meetings without any of the people who were involved in the day-to-day grind. Especially my dad, our brokers, and me. Frank and the board started yet another new plan for the business, and the first item on it was to get rid of us. Frank was a snake in the grass, a worm in the orchard. He was hired in the summer of 2014. At first, he was just biding his time. In 2015, he struck. He acted like he was trying to help me, I confided in him, and he used what I said in confidence against me. I was the first to see this, but it was too late, Frank had already sunk his teeth in.

LESSON LEARNED

Do not confide in strangers. You never know where they'll turn up in your life.

• •

I had accepted the award from CMU with pride and grace and gratitude, but to this day no one on the board has ever said a word about it to me, except for that one derogatory comment from Richard. I am proud of what we have accomplished. But my role at Michelle's Miracle has become increasingly unclear. Richard keeps saying "this company needs to move in a new direction," and that he is open to new ideas, but he is a terrible communicator and talks in circles. He has never once defined what "going in a new direction" means. I could not accept that this was not my company anymore. I was under the illusion that ownership percentage didn't matter, because we all supposedly still had a common goal: to make the company successful. But I was wrong. I'd lost my company years ago.

....

Bill again reminds me that all the word "fear" stands for is, "future events appearing real." My fears are: loss of income, loss of company, loss of house, loss of soul, and perhaps more than anything, loss of identity. When I am afraid, it is only physical activity that keeps me sober and keeps me sane. I had lost all faith.

I have spent the last three days working the July harvest on a friend's family cherry farm. My passion for cherries has been elevated beyond my dreams by seeing how they grow and how they are harvested. Every second that I spend in the orchards, I am in awe. First, I help skim leaves from the tanks and drive the tractor through the fields. Then I pick up the tank with the tractor—on the first try!—and set it down on the pad right where it needs to be. And last, I drive a 1984 Ford long bed with a trailer and five tanks equaling 10,000 pounds to the receiving station. The farm's motto is, "No thrill, No spill." I stay steady on the road—that was a precious cargo behind me—and have such a feeling of accomplishment when the cherries are safely unloaded. Most of all, I have fun. I can't remember when work felt so great or when I felt so appreciated.

The exhilaration of doing actual farm work has stuck with me and helps me realize how joyless my seemingly endless days at the company have become. My insomnia is back, and I wake up almost every night and write a list of everything I need to do that day at work. Prepare for a conference call. Ask Frank about our website. Work on a calendar with Frank. Catch up on company email. Learn Hootsuite. Pay bills. Plan trip to Detroit, and on, and on, and on.

I don't know why my mind is so awake. I don't know why my

body is so achy all the time. I try to trust that all is as it should be, that I am creating and manifesting abundance in wealth, health, peace, and helping others. I know it does not happen overnight, and I know it takes work, but I have been at it for more than ten years. It is now 2015! It is already spring. Before the summer is out, I will turn fifty.

The board does not understand why our sales are so low, but I do. Practically all of our marketing money has been pulled, and we still have not actually marketed to the consumer. We have only been spending marketing and advertising on the trade, but that only gets a product onto the shelf, it is not what gets a product off the shelf. Is this really what I want to be doing with the next half of my life? When I'm home, I'm so creative—with cooking our meals, with having dinner with my parents (and trying my best not to fight with them about the company, we were all under so much stress), making art, and even being creative with my gardening. But when I walk in the door at work, I feel my creativity is instantly stifled.

I pray for guidance. *Please, God, help me to see my life's purpose and help those in my life to recognize me, and recognize my gifts. Let me receive all the favors you have in store for me, and let others respect me as one of your children. Let me have the drive and the energy to do what I must. Amen.*

....

I wake up the next morning and make a promise to myself and to my creator to stay positive. If not for the whole day, then at least on my drive into Traverse City. In service to that ideal, I decide to take my camera and stop on the way and snap some cherry blossom pictures. They will look lovely on our website. I stop just before Hohnke Road on Route 651 and get out of my car. I walk over to the side of the road and take two pictures. But then I turn to the right and my car is not there.

That is because it is rolling down 651, heading south in the northbound lane!

I chase it down and jump into the driver's seat and stomp hard on the brakes seconds before the car veers into a ditch. This is my new company car, the one Richard picked out for me; I'd lost so much control I couldn't even pick out my own car, and here I was so distracted I almost let it wreck itself. How would I ever explain this to him?

This is a metaphor for my life. I want to spend it creating beauty, but instead I am careening dangerously in the wrong direction. I cannot do this for even one more day, and Bill is pushing me to see a doctor. I was not feeling well at all. I thought I could power through. Then, with my doctor's directive, I email Richard that I have been to a doctor, that I am extremely anemic and will be on a doctor's leave for the next week. That week turns into a two-week sabbatical, so that I can get a handle on my stress. Richard responded with one sentence: "You need to be more specific." I was already on sick leave and did not respond back. He never asked or said anything about it to me again. As a matter of fact, I hardly talked to him at all after Frank came on board.

I spend this needed time resting, crying, taking our dogs for walks, cuddling with Bill, writing letters to Sam and Randy at college, painting, and sitting outside and reading through my journals and crying some more. While I read, crows, cardinals, cottontails, and a fox all come into our yard. To me these creatures reflect renewal, creativity, new life, and strength. I haven't talked to my parents all week, and that feels okay. I am almost fifty years old, and I am finally feeling what it is like to think for myself. I notice a few things about my past journals. One, I tried to be the best mom I could with what I knew. Two, I spent a lot of time beating myself up about my drinking. And three, I am increasingly serious—really serious—about becoming a writer.

I also notice that through the years I've been saying the same things over and over. I want simple living. I've been worried about money my whole life. My current position has outgrown me or else I've outgrown it. It is truly time to separate myself from the company. It is no longer my company anyway; it is an entity with several disengaged people making decisions. The company does not need me. It needs a strong team, and instead, it's falling apart. Frank sold the board on a "new" marketing plan, which were really just my ideas he tried to take credit for. The plan was never enacted, I do not know why, but I do know Frank is trying to replace all the staff so he can seize control of the company. I'm on sick leave for stress; what more needs to be said?

· ·

On June 15, 2015, with Bill strongly supportive of me, I resign as president of Michelle's Miracle. I also resign my seat on the board of directors. That evening, I sit outside and look at the stars and, for just a minute I let this idea wash over me in the dark.

> *June 15, 2015*
>
> *To All Concerned Parties,*
>
> *In 1999 I was the first person to retail Tart Cherry Con-centrate (starting at a processing plant). At that time the government was paying farmers to throw their cherries on the ground,*
> *as there was no demand.*
>
> *In 2001, I started Leland Cherry Company: later to become Michelle's Miracle. I discovered tart cherries could be marketed for arthritis and gout and had a vision to help people feel better, as well as participate in*

LESSON LEARNED

Do not ever resign from a board seat on your own company. Even if you feel you must quit your job, keep your board seat. It is your only way of retaining any say or knowledge in decisions.

Farmland Preservation. At that time, very few knew of the many health benefits of tart cherries, but we persevered and created a retail category that previously did not exist, and more importantly, a demand for tart cherries.

It has been an experience of a lifetime and I am grateful to you all for your continued support! However, as exciting and challenging as the past 14 years have been, they have also taken a toll on my health, both emotionally and physically. I believe the best strategy for the company is for me to resign as President, CEO, and Board Member.

I would be honored to continue on a contract basis as the Founder, spokesperson, and face of the company, as these are my best strengths and I believe the company will benefit greatly; my passion for tart cherries will never waiver.

I see this as a positive move for Michelle's Miracle to succeed and become profitable with options for growth and/or an exit plan.

I truly feel this is the best solution for the company and for all who depend on its success.

Thank you!

Sincerely,

Michelle White

Founder, Michelle's Miracle and the Cherry Works Brand

It is going to get better I just know it.

••

The board retains me as spokesperson; my new role lasts only eighteen months, and I walk away completely from the company that bears my name. Once you sell off too many pieces of yourself, there isn't anymore "you" there, and the best course of action is just to leave . . . completely. The power struggles, the money grabs, the columns and columns of numbers, and the profit and loss statements are not for me. When I think of them, my heart pounds and my head hurts. Bill says my eyebrows are furrowed all the time.

All I was able to do was tell people about the healing power of this tiny red fruit that grows so perfectly in the sandy coastal soils of my beloved northern Michigan. I did that, to my best ability. And I was the first to do it.

As I reflect on my years at Michelle's Miracle, I feel pride and a sense of accomplishment. I created a new category of product that had never been retailed before, and more importantly, I created a demand for tart cherries. Building and growing this company has been an experience of a lifetime, and I am grateful to everyone who had a hand in that accomplishment, from Bill, my parents, and Smitty, our first employee, and everyone thereafter.

Each one of them played a role in the company and in my life. Some were guides to what to do and how to live, and some were the opposite. I learned something from all of them, and for that, I am grateful.

Now I am ready to look and see what the second half of my life will be about. I feel that this is a positive move for me and for the company. I have been searching and searching for so long, for money, for success, and for recognition of a job well done.

The miracle is not the company. The miracle is in the fruit that God created and shared with man.

What I've learned on my travels has surprised me.

I've learned that what I am looking for is not out there; it is in me. And at this point in my life, I need to take the time to look inside myself and, with the support of my husband and my sons, find out what it is.

Harvest

2016

ICHIGAN IS KNOWN FAR AND WIDE FOR THE BEAUTIFUL FALL COLORS the trees put on display every fall. The flashiest trees are the sugar maples, with their bright reds and pinks. Next in line are the poplar trees, sometimes called aspens, with their electric yellow leaves that whisper in the slightest breeze. Tart cherry trees offer a fragrant display in the spring, but they don't stand out in October and November. Their leaves turn a flat gold, and then a dark reddish-brown color, before falling to the ground and creating a natural layer of mulch in the orchard.

I fully resigned from the company I had started, on October 30, 2016. Richard had wanted out, too, and replaced himself by yet another CEO, this one named Meghan. She had her own series of meaningless criticisms to level against the company, the management, and me. My last day was November 11. That date was meaningful to me—the eleventh day of the eleventh month. All those 1's were symbols of my new beginning. I still owned stock in what had once been "my" company, but that was my only tie. I wasn't sure what I'd do about that—and I chose not to decide right away. I had the luxury of thinking about things now, before I made decisions.

Even after all that has happened, cherry trees are still my favorite trees of all. That's because I know that what is on the outside doesn't always tell you everything that's on the inside. And every fall, my daily walks take me, sometimes subconsciously, through nearby orchards. Sometimes with my dogs and Bill, and other times, alone. It's where this whole story began and where I still find a certain sense of peace I cannot get anywhere else.

I've been writing and painting. I've been cooking and writing down recipes, many with cherries as one of the main ingredients. I've been reading and spending time with Bill. Not hurry-up time, but time to linger over good conversations and memories of our life together so far. I've been visiting Sam and Randy. And I've been thinking. Reflecting on my life and finding meaning in my choices. I have time to do all of this now that I am not chasing the next round of funding, or sitting in an airport somewhere, laptop open, headphones on, preparing to make one more presentation. I have greatly reduced my stress and anxiety. For so many years keeping a business going, while trying to navigate around the toxic personalities who had taken over my company, had been my focus. I accepted, and then rejoiced, that such things were not my focus anymore. Once I was able to do that, the anxiety plaguing me for so long simply faded away.

Last week Bill and I had dinner with my parents. It was so good to see them! Then after the meal, my dad made the comment that there was a lot going on at the company, but that the plans were still in flux so he couldn't talk about them. I surprised myself by saying, "Okay," and meaning it. I hope there is a lot going on at the company, I really do; it's just that it doesn't concern me anymore, so I find myself not feeling responsible or caring what it is. I think this attitude surprised my dad, too. The Michelle of a couple months ago would have tried and tried to drag it out of him.

Those last years at the company robbed me of my creativity and my soul, and I am just now getting that part of myself back. If I let myself get drawn in again, my creativity will recede once more, and I refuse to let that happen. I missed that part of me, I was not a whole person without it, and it has taken a lot of writing and painting and praying to encourage it to return.

After my parents left, Bill and I went for a walk with our dog, Charlie. On the way home, we saw the most amazing sunset. It was like a beam of light was shining straight down to earth from the sky. The sun was a stunning color and the beam looked just like a cross of light, and then it slowly changed colors and faded away. The company meant so much to me that while working for its success, I lost who I was.

Although the company started out as my dream, the harder I tried to keep to my mission, the more I'd been forced to let go of it in order to raise money. In the process, I had forgotten how creative I truly was. Today I feel a sense of happiness and peace at the thought of being able to spend the next fifty years writing, painting, and cooking. I will help people and inspire them, but on my terms and no one else's. I'm not sure what that will be yet, but I know it will be.

Tomorrow is a new day. Tomorrow is the start of the next part of my life and the next part of my story. That story begins with, "She was herself, every day and always, and she has a new best friend, God!" Then a bunch of exciting, fun, and adventuresome things will happen, and when the story ends, if it ends, I already know it will end like this: "Then she lived happily ever after. No matter what."

*L*IFE FEELS EFFORTLESS.

I don't mean that everything comes easy to me now. That would not only be unrealistic, but unsatisfying, too. I mean that I have begun to feel a natural internal pull, a guiding energy that aims me in the right direction, even when things are challenging or difficult. I know myself. I know my strengths, but I know my weaknesses, too. I jump with both feet into the things I'm good at and hand off the rest to people who are good at those tasks that I am not.

After I left the company, my friends, my family, and even some of my former co-workers asked: "Michelle, what are you going to do now?" "I am going to heal," I told them. And, I have.

In December 2016, I still owned stock in the company, so I was invited to the annual meeting with all the other investors. I asked to be put on the agenda; I wanted to discuss the state of the company, and I wanted to do it publicly. This was not a popular idea with anyone but Bill and I, and an alternative was proposed. Mr. George's son and the company CEO would meet with me two hours prior to the board meeting. "You will have our undivided attention," the CEO promised. Bill warned me that their motives were insincere, and I agreed, but I agreed to meet with them anyway.

I just wanted to be heard. Isn't that what everyone in a conflict wants?

The day came, and Bill and I sat on one side of a long table, Mr. George's CEO was on the end of the table by me, and Mr. George's son sat across from us. I wanted to share my thoughts about the future of the company. The

things we'd done right and the things we'd done wrong. Inside, I was still trying to recover from all the demeaning things Richard had said to me in the months before I'd resigned. I wanted to talk about that, too, but it would be impossible.

The meeting between the four of us did not go well. I didn't feel listened to at all, but Bill and I did attend the board meeting afterwards. I thought I could share my thoughts there, but when I tried to speak, that effort didn't go well, either. I was shaking, feeling distraught, and in order to keep my thoughts straight, I read a letter I'd written ahead of time instead of speaking off the cuff. My words were soon overshadowed by my years of anger and frustration.

A year passed. I still owned company stock, and Bill and I again attended the annual board meeting. We walked into the room together and sat at the end of a very large, handmade, triangle-shaped table.

This time, I felt calm and ready.

I had repeatedly requested copies of the financial statements and the budget, and they'd been emailed. I'd tried to review them, but the figures were almost incomprehensible. When the meeting began, Meghan went quickly through the financial statements, frequently looking up at Bill and I, and asking, "Do you have any questions?" "No," I answered, anxious for her to get to the budget.

Finally, she did.

"How is the company going to make money if expenses are

almost as high as the gross margin, and if there's almost nothing budgeted for advertising?" I asked.

My ability to handle the finances had been roundly criticized by the board when I was CEO, and yet I'd worked for weeks putting the annual budget together. This document looked like it had been hurriedly drafted five minutes before. There was no real-world distribution at all; they were putting all their hopes on the Internet.

"How are you going to drive sales to the website, if no one knows the website exists?" I wanted to know. They had no answer.

"You don't think we have enough in marketing, do you?" Meghan asked.

"No, I don't, and your professional fees are way too high."

The board ignored these issues and continued instead to tout the power of using social media to drive online sales. If that was the case, I said, then now would be a good time to have every-one get on their phones and go to the website and click on the Instagram icon. This was the last week of December; the most recent Instagram post, which everyone could plainly see, had been made by me. In October 2016.

There was a pause, and I know exactly what the members of the board felt in that moment. Embarrassment, defeat, and a feeling of being overwhelmed by how much there was to do. At least, that's what I would have felt in their shoes. I used to feel those emotions every single day for years.

"Okay," Meghan said. "Point made."

By the time Bill and I left the meeting, someone had logged into the website and removed the Instagram icon. Today, it's still missing and the website looks like it's having a fire sale. Every-thing must go!

This had been a complex moment for me. I was sad to see the diminishment of the company I'd built, yet also comforted to realize I was not the cause of it. That moment freed me in a way that nothing else did. For the first time since 2003, I was not afraid, I was confident, and I didn't care what they said to me! It was the best and strangest feeling to finally see it all for what it was, and not take any of it personally.

When I first resigned back in November 2016, one of the things I did to heal myself was join up with some other women artists to paint, have discussions about life, and delve into our spirituality. I was reading a lot then, and I asked these women if they belonged to a book club. They said not per se, but they did discuss books at their Tuesday Bible study group. "You should come," they said.

That's not for me, I thought. I believe in God—I think—but I'm not a Bible thumper.

The very next Tuesday, I found myself walking up the street to Bible study. And it has changed my life. I used to pray, but I didn't really believe. Now that I can see clearly, I have found a true faith and I am on a different, and right, path. So much so, I felt a calling from God and have been on track to become a deaconess for the United Methodist Church. I have been taking supplies to make art projects to an outreach program for home-less and marginalized people. In them I have found God, art, peace and purpose, and nothing has made more sense to me! I have found there to be more dignity and compassion working in the outreach program than any board room meeting I have ever been in.

Bill always said, "If you believe, you will achieve." Now I know what he meant.

My parents are no longer with the company, either. My dad, at seventy-five years old, has started a new business, and he and my mom are busy living their lives. They have taught me that there is no time for grass to grow under our feet. The three of us were the core team at the company for years. It was our idea, we founded it, we worked to build it, and for too many years it even seemed to take precedence over us being a family.

Those anxious days are behind us now. We are a family again.

No more fighting, no more fear, and no more deception. Peace and love is what we live for. Now and always.

Occasionally, I'll think of that day in July 2004 when I pulled my car over and was contemplating opening the door into traffic. I have so much compassion for the woman I was. And when the words, down the road, pop into my head these days, it means it's time for Bill and me to take a walk with our dogs. To notice the scenery. To stop and smell the cherry trees. To thank God for all that we are to each other and for all that we have been given. May it ever be so.

PHOTOS & POEMS

Ironic that the sign I stand in front of
as a little girl would say "Peddler" on it.
I loved "peddling" cherry juice concentrate.

SPRING ARBOR UNIVERSITY
Commencement Ceremony
June 1, 2002

*At 36 years I finally obtained a degree in Family Life
Education. As I walk into a new life I am so glad I went for
this field as it will serve me well going forward.*

Right after the Marathon we all gathered. I was so excited to be with my family and exhausted after running for 5 hours 7 minutes and 20 seconds.

*My confirmation with Pastor Pool, he has since passed
but never forgotten.*

Above: My beautiful mom and I at our wedding.

Previous page: Dad smiling like a Cheshire cat.

Our amazing wedding... That's me taller and Bill already getting used to it.

FOR MICHELLE

Come walk with me
    My partner in life
Come walk with me
    And be my wife

Our laughter and tears
    We will share
As we face life
    Forever a pair

My lover, my partner
    Forever a friend
A future together —
    Journey without end

Come walk with me
    My partner in life
Come walk with me
    And be my wife

— Bill White

Photo by Jane Louise Bourrow

Standing left to right: Bill White, John Vidergar and Craig Smith. Seated are Michelle White and Gail Vidergar.

Top: Our first farm market, at that time we still had Amon Orchards on our marketing material.

Bottom: Our first full staff media photo. That was the core team from beginning to end. We were all so full of hope and excitement.

Me in the very cherry kitchen whipping up all kinds of cherry goodies.

2010

MICHELLE WHITE of Leland received this award from the Leelanau Horticulture Society for her contributions to the fruit industry. White is the owner and president of Michelle's Miracle, Inc.

White is honored by Horticultural Society

Michelle White of Leland, the founder of president of Michelle's Miracle, Inc., has been honored by the Leelanau Horticultural Society for her contributions to the fruit industry.

White was named the 2010 recipient of the society's Distinguished Service Award. She has been a longtime advocate of Michigan's cherry industry, and in 2001 founded the Leland Cherry Company. In 2008, when Michelle's Miracle was formed, the Leland Cherry Company was merged into the new company.

Michelle's Miracle manufactures and sells branded and private label tart cherry nutraceutical products to wholesale, retail and e-commerce customers worldwide. More information about the company is available at www.michellesmiracle.com.

White said that among the ways she supports Michigan's cherry-farming industry is by working to preserve farmland and developing products that provide healthy and natural nutrients to consumers. Michelle's Miracle also donates a portion of the company's sales to the Leelanau Conservancy.

"Cherry farmland in northern Michigan is currently more valuable for building superstores and subdivisions than growing cherries because global markets pay little for the state's farm products," she said. "Bringing Michigan farmers closer to consumer markets may be one of the best courses of action for global growth of Michigan's second-largest industry."

146

Facing page: The Horticultural Society award.

Above: Bill and I at the CMU–RC award night. He was so proud.

Facing page, top: Fox News.
Bottom: Lovey Copper (made by Sarah Mead-Wall) went everywhere
with me for a while until Frank came up with his own doll but she
never made it out of the box it was so bad.

Above: Fox news — I loved doing live television and talking about the
health benefits while making great recipes with cool people.

*Me feeling free and excited in Tucson. I had made up my mind
to progress into the Deaconess program.*

THE NEW YOU

I'm beginning to see
    The passion in you

As you face life
    With eyes anew

Facing new challenges
    With soul revived

You travel this road
    Your spirit alive

Improving your mind
    Improving your soul

Improving yourself
    Becomes your goal

Have no regrets
    Always let it be said

You did it for you
    To get ahead

— Bill White

I ONCE KNEW A LADY

I once knew a lady
    brown eyes and brown hair
Her skin so soft
    — complexion so fair.

I once knew a lady
    so fair and so fine
Her presence complements
    like a fine wine.

I once knew a lady
    whose child within
Struggled to find
    innocence again.

I once knew a lady
    I'd only seen
At night when I slept
    then only a dream.

A lady with beauty
    hidden deep inside
Whose spirit was free
    it can't be denied.

I once knew a lady
    her passion denied
Suppressed for the moment
    and yet still alive.

A passion that burns
     intent to be free
A passion for years
      no one could see.

A passion intense
     held deep inside
For fear of the moment
      It won't be denied.

I now know a lady
     not only a dream
A lady whose beauty
     I'd never seen.

Oh lady, my lady
     if never I see
The passion within
     from you set free.

Oh lady, my lady
     please listen to me
Love yourself first
     and you will be free.

I once knew a lady
     a lady I knew
I once knew a lady
     a spirit so true.

— *Bill White*

UNCONDITIONAL

Unconditional, she said to me,
That's how my love would have to be.

Let your feelings for me be free,
Let life be what it is to be.

Do not judge me or demand,
Take me just the way I am.

For if our love is not to end,
Just stand by me and be my friend.

This painful love I feel for you,
Is something that I never knew.

No matter where our lives will end,
You'll always be a cherished friend.

For you helped me feel and to love,
Oh what a beautiful feeling — love!

— *Bill White*

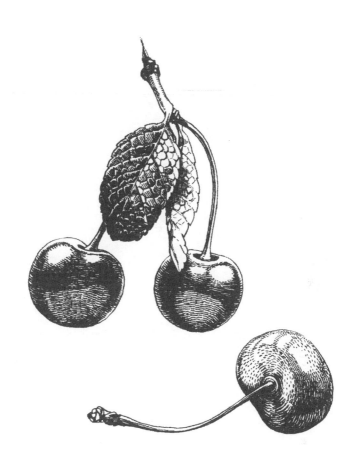

27679436R00102

Made in the USA
Lexington, KY
07 January 2019